our historic
BOUNDARY WATERS
from lake superior to lake of the woods

by Dr. Duane R. Lund

Distributed by

Adventure Publications
P.O. Box 269
Cambridge, Minnesota 55008

Printed by

Nordell Graphic Communications, Inc
Staples, Minnesota 56479

ISBN 0-934860-13-0

TABLE OF CONTENTS

1st Printing, 1980
2nd Printing, 1981
3rd Printing, 1983
4th Printing, 1986
5th Printing, 1988
6th Printing, 1991
7th Printing, 1993
8th Printing, 2000

Copyright © 1980 by
Dr. Duane R. Lund
Staples, MN 56479

Printed in the United States of America

CHAPTER ONE
Canoe Country - Indian Country

It was so long ago we aren't even certain of the date - but it was probably in 1688 or 1689 when a young, twenty-year old French Canadian, Jacques De Noyon, swung the prow of his canoe around the last bend in the Rainy River and gazed out onto the Lake of the Woods, thus becoming the first white man to completely traverse the area about which this book has been written, namely; the waterways and portages which join Lake Superior with the Lake of the Woods.

Others may have gone part way or crossed this maize of lakes and streams while traveling north or south. Seventeenth Century missionaries and traders really got around - some without reporting or even knowing where they had been. We do know, for example, that missionaries arrived at the huge Ojibway village at Sault Ste. Marie[1] in 1640. Radisson and Groseilliers were on the Great Lakes in 1660, and ventured south into what is now Wisconsin and possibly even into Minnesota.[2]

In 1679, David Greysolon, the sieur du Lhut, probably visited Grand Portage as he moved along the north shore of Lake Superior. No doubt many traders and trappers worked their way west into our *Canoe Country* from this base of operations.

But as far as we know, it was De Noyon, a youthful trader and trapper barely out of his "teens" who was the first white man to explore and enjoy the immense beauty of the entire length of the Minnesota-Ontario boundary waters - including the Canadian Quetico, the American wilderness canoe area, Voyageurs National Park, and farther west down the Rainy River to Lake of the Woods. He probably gave little thought to those who would follow, but thousands were destined to experience the joys and hardships of this wilderness wonderland: other traders and trappers, missionaries, explorers, voyageurs, prospectors, lumberjacks, and many in recent years like you and I who have come to re-create mind and body. Miraculously, the same natural beauty has welcomed all of us. Some of the identical virgin White and Norway pines that watch us pass also looked down on the voyageurs! But De Noyon was first. And we think, "How brave; how daring; what an achievement!" And it was. But we so often forget that white man was really a "Johnny-come-lately" on the scene. To the Indians who guided De

[1]The village eventually reached a population of about 2000 in 1680 when it was the unofficial capital of the Ojibway Nation.

[2]According to the descriptions in Radisson's diary and Indian tradition, the traders may have penetrated as far west as Knife Lake, just north of Mille Lacs Lake.

Noyon, the portages, streams, and lakes were as familiar as the nearest freeway is to us. After all, they and their ancestors had called this "home" for generations.[1] Archeologists estimate that white man's involvement here is only 5% of human history in the region. How unfair of us to consider everything as beginning with his arrival on the scene -

So when really did the first man (or woman?) enter this wilderness paradise?

Was the first person a lone scout looking for a more productive area for hunting and trapping?

Was it a family fleeing hostile neighbors?

Or was it an entire tribe on the move, searching for an easier life?

We will never know, but we do know that man came here several thousands of years before De Noyon's adventure. A hand-worked piece of antler has been found near Lake of the Woods (Morson, Ontario) which radiocarbon tests[2] indicate could be 8000 years old. Artifacts made of live ivory and found in burial mounds in the area indicate that these first residents were contemporary with the wooly mammoth. They probably also hunted such prehistoric game as the giant bison with their leaf-shaped spears. Further evidence of man's early arrival on the scene in this area are copper artifacts unearthed from burial mounds and estimated to be 4000 years old. This would make them the oldest man-made implements found thus far on either North or South America.[3] All of which means that the early inhabitants of this continent followed not too far behind the last receding glacier (the fourth) as it melted its way north.

We are told these glaciers once covered Minnesota and Ontario with compacted snow and ice as much as one mile thick. As the glacier moved, it ground boulder against boulder and gouged out the irregular terrain we see today. At first, except for the abundance of water, our boundary area must have looked much like a moon-scape, completely void of vegetation or life. But as fish and plant life returned and birds once again found food and shelter, animals and man, himself, moved north. The region surely looked quite different than it does today. The western portion was a part of the great Lake Agassiz - the giant body of water created by the melting of the glacier and which included the Red Lakes of Minnesota to the south and Lakes Winnipeg and Manitoba to the north and a total area larger than the Great Lakes, combined. The area east and north of Rainy River is in sharp contrast to the flat, loamy land that was once the floor of Lake Agassiz; it is characterized instead by rough outcroppings of granite from the Laurentian Shield. The rivers and lakes of our *Canoe Country* did not assume their present identities or shorelines until sometime between 2000 BC and the time of Christ.

Where did the first inhabitants of our *Canoe Country* come from? We know that

---

[1]Actually, many of the Indians may have been relatively new to the area. The Ojibway infiltrated the region in the 1600's as they fled before the Iroquois unslaught from the east.

[2]It should be noted that the accuracy of radiocarbon tests has been challenged in recent years.

[3]Dr. Walter Kenyon excavated copper artifacts (including a gaff) at Pither's Point on Rainy Lake in 1959 and other copper items were found at Houska's Point (Ranier), also on Rainy Lake. Gold art work found in South and Central America may be older; but these are probably the oldest metal tools and weapons.

they were of the Indian race and that their ancestors probably crossed the Bering Straights, coming into what is now Alaska from their original homes in Asia. Present day archeologists believe they then migrated down the west coast of North America and later moved in a north-westerly direction across the continent. Although Indian tribes are generally believed to have been nomadic in nature, they would settle in certain areas for generations, and the more ideal village sites saw different tribes come and go over the centuries. This is also true of our border region. "Cemeteries" of burial mounds and single gigantic mounds which probably contained the bones of several generations, indicate that certain tribes may have settled here for relatively long periods of time. In 1844, George Bryce[1] reported twenty-four of these larger mounds along the Rainy River. There are five mounds on the American side at the mouth of the Big Fork at Laurel. Another large mound at Pike Bay of Lake Vermilion is also believed to be of this culture.

These larger mounds (some are as much as forty feet high and over 100 feet in length) are associated with a later people whom the archeologists have labeled "the Laurel Culture," who probably came into *Canoe Country* sometime before the birth of Christ. They were possibly the first to bring the bow and arrow into this region - and may have come (directly or indirectly) from the Pacific coast or the Gulf of Mexico. At any rate, shell ornaments found in their burial mounds are of that origin. Other artifacts found include sheet copper, decorated pieces of pottery, harpoons, and a variety of projectile heads. The bones were buried in bundles, indicating that the bodies were probably placed in trees or on scaffolds or in shallow graves to decompose before burial. The marrow had been removed from the larger bones and the brains removed from some of the skulls soon after death. In some cases, the eye sockets were filled with clay. Some archeologists have concluded there may have been certain canibalistic rituals following a death. Nothing is known of what happened to these people; they just disappeared.

Many archeologists believe that the earliest mound builders in this part of the continent were the Hopewell Indians of southern Minnesota. Northern tribes may have learned from them.

Sometime around 1000 A.D. a new people arrived in northern Minnesota and established what we have labeled as the "Blackduck Culture."[2] Whether they pushed the Laurel people out or assimilated them is not known, perhaps some of each. The Blackduck people buried their dead in pits and then built mounds over the remains. Two such burial mounds, dated around 1200 A.D. and located at the mouth of the Rainy River, contained a spectacular find: seven skulls—modeled and decorated with paint, as well as a variety of ornaments, pipes, shells, antlers, etc. The Blackduck culture prevailed until the 17th century in the woodlands of Minnesota.

Also around 1000 A.D. another Indian civilization, known as the "Mississippi Culture" moved into sourthern Minnesota from the south and southwest. Among them were tribes of the Sioux Nation, including the Dakotas. It is possible, however, that

[1]Bryce, George. The Lake of the Woods, its History, Geology, Mining and Manufacturing, Toronto Free Press, 1897

[2]Both the Laurel and Blackduck cultures are also referred to as "Woodland cultures."

other Sioux tribes were already here.

The Sioux knew something about agriculture and were particularly dependent on maize (Indian corn). The fact that maize did not grow well in the colder climate of northern Minnesota was one of the reasons the Mississippi Culture did not move north of an imaginary line between the present site of Minnesota's Twin Cities and Lake Traverse (until the 17th century). During the 1600's, however, the Sioux came to dominate all but the extreme far north of the Minnesota region. They never did gain control of the border area, but they surely tried. During the latter half of the 17th century, the Ojibway began their migration from the east into our state.

Sioux Teepees

Included sometime in the pre-Dakota era was a tribe called "Gros Ventre"[1] by the French. They were a remarkable people. Eventually pushed west into the Dakotas, they established their earthen dwellings in villages on the banks of the Missouri River near the Mandans. The tribes grew quite similar over the years. The Mandans probably also came by way of Minnesota and some anthropologists feel the two tribes are related. Both peoples placed a high priority on cleanliness and were known to bathe twice a day, using a white clay as a cleansing agent. Ojibway visitors to the Gros Ventres in the 1800's were impressed with their knowledge of the Minnesota lakes region and were shown a map of sorts on birch bark which included Sandy Lake. Nearly wiped out by smallpox and war parties, other tribes developed a sympathy for them and eventually offered them protection.[2]

Our boundary waters canoe area was inhabited by the Cree, the Ottawa, the Ojibway, and the Assiniboin during the years when white men explored the region. The Cree, Ottawa and Ojibway were Algonquin tribes with roots farther east. The Assiniboin were a part of the Sioux Nation and had originally moved into southern Wisconsin from farther south or southwest. They did not get along with their Sioux cousins - the Winnebagos -and fled to this northern region. Literally, their name means "Sioux of the

Ojibway lodge - covered with bark and hides

[1] The Ojibway called them "the ancient people."

[2] Warren, William, History of the Ojibways, Minn. Historical Collection, Vol. 5.

rocks" or "snakes of the rocks." (As the Ojibway learned to dislike the Sioux, they began referring to them as "snakes.")[1] Because of their common dislike for the other Sioux tribes, the Cree, Ojibway, and Assiniboin formed an alliance and successfully kept the Dakotas out of the Lake of the Woods and boundary waters area. In the 1700's, the allies raided Sioux villages to the south and west, including some located on Minnesota's Red Lakes. But the Sioux (Dakotas) were also devastating in their raids on the northland. It was the Sioux who massacred Jean Baptiste La Verendye, Father Alneau, and 19 soldier-voyageurs on Lake of the Woods in 1734.

Eventually, (by 1770), the Alliance drove the Dakota Sioux out of their woodland strongholds, but the Ojibway and the Sioux continued their struggle for more than 100 years, almost up to the time of the Civil War. Although the Sioux were routed from their woodland villagesby 1770, raids and counter-raids continued. Prior to 1770, northern Minnesota was a virtual "no man's land" for more than thirty years with the Ojibway launching attacks from what is now Wisconsin, the Sioux attacking from southern and western Minnesota, and the Cree, Assiniboin and Ojibway launching raids from the border country. By the 1800's, the Assiniboin had moved to Lake Winnipeg and eventually farther west to the Canadian plains and foothills; likewise, the Ottawa. Large numbers of the Cree moved north into Ontario and northwest into Manitoba, leaving mostly Ojibwas in our present day "Canoe Country."

The major Indian tribes of North America were distinctly different from each other. Their differences went beyond customs and traditions; they were also different in physical appearance and in language. The Sioux, for example, were taller and leaner than the Ojibway. Apparently they came from different ancestoral stock because there was little similarity in their language; even the root words were quite different. They may well have come from different parts of Asia. Difficulty in communication among the Indian peoples no doubt contributed to the inter-tribal hostility.

The following table may be helpful in understanding the different origins and relationships of the several tribes which occupied the eastern half of what is now Canada and the United States at the time of the settlement of the eastern seaboard by European immigrants:

SIOUX		**ALGONQUIN**	**IROQUOIS**
Dakota (with seven	Oto	Ojibway[2] (Chippewa)	Mohawk
Sisseton councils)	Missouri	Ottawa	Oneida
Teton	Omaha	Sac	Onondaga
Yankton	Osage	Fox	Cayuga
Yanktonai	Ponca	Potawatomi	Seneca
Wahpeton	Hidatsa	Illinois	(these five had a close
Wahpakute	Crow	Shawnee	Tuscarora alliance)
Mdewakanton	Mandan	Miami Menominees	Erie
Iowa	Assiniboin	Kickapoo Cree	Hurons
	Winnebago		

[1]The Sioux were also called "roasters."

[2]There are several acceptable spellings of "Ojibway" (Schoolcraft's spelling). The tribe was also called "Chippewa" perhaps a French corruption of "Ojibway." "Chippewa" often appears on treaties and other legal documents. Theories of the origin and meaning of the word include "to pucker" which could apply to the design of their moccasins or to the effect on the skins of their victims placed too close to the fire. They have sometimes called themselves "Anishinanbay."

In the 17th century, as the colonies were being established, the Iroquios inhabited the coastal area west to the Appalachians; the Sioux occupied the western part of the midwest, with some tribes found farther to the south and southwest; and the Algonquins were generally in between with a few tribes as far east as New England.[2] The individual sub-tribes were spread out within these general regions. The five tribes of the Iroquois Lodge (Oneida, Mohawk, Onondaga, Cayuga, and Seneca) were in and around what is now New York State. The Eries were along the coast; the Tuscarora to the south. The Hurons had their troubles with there Iroquois cousins and moved north. The hostility grew and a "Neutral Nation" was allowed to exist in between them as a buffer.

Among the tribes of the Sioux Nation, the Dakotas occupied present day Minnesota with the Assiniboins to the far north, the Winnebago to the east (Wisconsin), the Hidatsa, Crow, and Mandans to the west (Dakotas), and the others to the south (Oto, Ponca, Osage, Omaha, Iowa, and the Missouris).

The Algonquin tribes were generally scattered throughout the area between the Sioux and the Iroquois. The Ojibway were by far the largest of the Algonquin tribes. For an unknown length of time they were involved in "The Three Fires Confederacy" with the Ottawa and the Potawatomi. They separated, according to Ojibway tradition, about 400 years ago. The Ojibway covered an area so vast (particularly after they fled from the Iroquois) that they were sometimes described as four separate groups:

(1) Southeastern Ojibway or "Bungi" - between Lake Michigan & Lake Erie.

(2) Southwestern Ojibway - Wisconsin, the Michigan Peninsula and later - southern Minnesota.

(3) Northern Ojibway or Salteaux - Ontario and eventually northern Minnesota.

(4) Plains Ojibway - Manitoba and northern North Dakota.

Although there was, no doubt, a good deal of strife over the centuries between the various tribes and sub-tribes, the first extensive (recorded) warfare was in the late 1640's. Prior to that time the Indians did not have gunpowder and there seemed to be enough land with good hunting, fishing, and trapping for all. Early explorers reported considerable fighting among the Indians but it was usually on a small scale and usually seasonal. During the months of good hunting and harvesting there was little time for fighting. Winter made warfare most uncomfortable and the snow made tracking much too easy to carry out revenge. Then, too, cold and famine were the greater enemies that time of year. Yet, fighting and scalp-taking were very much a way of life. A good deal of bloodshed took place over hunting grounds, wild rice beds, and even over misunderstandings growing out of inter-tribal marriages and family spats. But most fighting was localized and between neighboring tribes.

As the colonists traded their guns and powder to the Indians, the stage was being set for inter-tribal warfare far more devastating. We have already told how the Hurons split off from the Iroquois Lodge and moved farther north. The day finally came when the "Neutral Nation" in between was not a sufficient buffer to prevent the well-armed Iroquis from launching an all out attack to rid themselves once and for all of their enemies. The five Iroquois allies, armed with weapons provided by the English, Dutch, and

[2]Ojibway tradition tells of when these people once lived by the Atlantic.

Swedish colonists, set out to annihilate the Hurons and anyone else suspected of aligning themselves with them - including the Eries, the Neutral Nation, the eastern Algonquins, and any Frenchmen who happened to become involved. Thousands[1] were scalped and mutilated. The survivors retreated where they could - west, and thus began the migration of the Ojibway towards their future home - Minnesota, Wisconsin, and Ontario.

Chippewa Scalp Dance - water color by Peter Rindisbacker   West Point Museum

   The Ojibway migration routes lead both north and south of Lake Superior; the majority chose the southern route and settled in Wisconsin. Those using the northern way settled along the north shore of Lake Superior and around Rainy Lake and the Lake of the Woods with a scattering of villages in between. Contrary to what we might expect, there was little confrontation at first between the Ojibway and the Sioux, even though they were traditional enemies. The basic reason was economic. The French needed the furs of the Minnesota Lake region and knew virtually none would be available if the Sioux and Ojibway were at war. The Sioux and the Ojibway realized too that there would be no trade items available to them if they had to spend their time defending themselves against each other instead of collecting furs. Du Luth was the chief negotiator and genuine hero of the peace-keeping effort. He wintered with the Ojibway at Sault Ste. Marie in 1678-79 and during that time developed a good working relationship with both the French traders and the Indians. With the coming of the ice break-up in the spring, Du Luth lead a band of Ojibway to a site near the city which now bears his name, and there held the council (which we mentioned in our opening paragraph) with several tribes in an attempt to expand the fur trade industry into Minnesota and southern Ontario. At this meeting, representatives of the Dakota, Cree and Assiniboin pledged friendship and cooperation with the French and Ojibway. No mean accomplishment! Du Luth also used the occasion to lay claim to the entire upper

[1]LaVérendye later suspected these men may have been bribed by his competitors.

Mississippi area for France. In the same year (1679), Du Luth founded a trading post on Lake Superior, possibly at Grand Portage. From this base he established trade with the Sioux tribes of the lake region with the Ojibway as the middlemen! Grand Portage was destined to become the rendezvous point for the voyageurs from Montreal ("porkeaters") and those from Lake Athabasca and other western points ("men of the north"). Because it was impossible to travel all the way from Montreal to the trading posts in the west and return in a single season, a meeting place was necessary for the exchange of furs and trade goods. Grand Portage was that place.

Trade developed rapidly. LaSalle reported in 1682 that the Ojibway were trading with the Dakotas as far as 150 miles to the west. The peaceful arrangement allowed large numbers of Ojibway to settle in Wisconsin and along the north and south shores of Lake Superior and as far west along the border country as the Lake of the Woods. But the peace was too good to last. With a history of tribal conflicts, fears and suspicions were latent in everyone's minds. Small incidents were quickly magnified and any death called for revenge. By 1730 the truce was an uneasy one.

This was the atmosphere that greeted the legendary French-Canadian explorer, Pierre La Verendrye, when he arrived at Grand Portage in 1731. Here, many of his men rebelled and refused to go farther. Because of the lateness of the season, the rugged country which lie ahead, and the uncertainties which awaited them, La Verendrye gave in and returned with most of his men to Fort Kaministikwia (later called Fort William) to spend the winter. But his nephew, La Jemeraye, and his oldest son, Jean Baptiste, continued on with a smaller group (perhaps volunteers) through our "Canoe Country" and built a fort at the west end of Rainy Lake (Fort St. Pierre). Come spring, La Verendrye went on to Lake of the Woods, where he built historic Fort St. Charles and began an adventure as exciting as any fiction ever written. But now we are getting ahead of our story; Chapter Two will deal with the explorers, traders, trappers, and missionaries as they came to our "Canoe Country." So, first, let us get better acquainted with the people who welcomed and guided the white men: the Algonquin tribes of the American Indian.

The "Canoe Country" was an attractive homeland for anyone who was at the mercy of "Mother Nature" for survival. Food was plentiful during most months of the year. Lakes and streams had a bountiful supply of trout, whitefish, sturgeon, walleyes, bass, northerns, crappies, as well as less desireable varieties of fish. Thousands of acres of wild rice provided an important and all-purpose vegetable product; the rice also was an attraction for waterfowl, which meant tasty meat for the Indian's diet. The woodlands were a dependable source of berries and nuts of many kinds. The forests also provided partridges, sprucehens, passenger pigeons and other birds for food as well as animal life which in turn gave the Indian both meat and clothing.

The boundary waters were not blessed with as large maple forests (sugar bush) as those found so abundantly farther south, but the Indians here did have access to the sugar and syrup produced from the sap of these beautiful trees.

Permanent lodges were located in the maple groves for use each spring. They were large, usually measuring from 10 to 20 feet wide and 25 to 40 feet long. Sometimes smaller, temporary huts were built - called "wig-wa-si-ga-mig" by the Ojibway. Whites nicknamed them "wigwams." The trees were tapped by cutting a slash and driving a cedar splinter or carved spigot into the wood. The sap dripped off the splinter and was then collected in containers on the ground (made from birchbark). Syrup was made by boiling the sap for days over an open fire.[1] Although the syrup was sometimes used for food, it was usually thickened by continued boiling and then when it was the right consistency, placed in a basswood trough where it was gently stirred until it became granulated, thus forming sugar.

Ojibway Sugar Camp Wigwam   Courtesy Minnesota Historical Society

Often times the syrup was poured into molds and allowed to harden. This "hard sugar" could be stored more conveniently for use throughout the year. One family could prepare as much as 500 pounds of maple sugar in a single season. The hard sugar was eaten as a food or confection; granulated sugar was used as a seasoning or flavoring agent; and a beverage was made by dissolving the maple sugar in water.

Spring was also the time for fishing, trapping, and hunting. In addition to using nets and traps, spawning fish were often speared at night with a birch bark or pine knot torch for light. Migratory waterfowl were again found on the Indian menu. Muskrats were easier to trap. All in all, spring was a time both for work and rejoicing. Celebrations, feasting and religious ceremonies accompanied the spring activities.

July and August were a season for berry picking. The braves may have been helpful in locating the berry patches, but the women and children did the picking. Just as today, the woodlands of Minnesota and Ontario had an abundance of blueberries, chokecherries, pincherries, blackberries, raspberries, strawberries, and cranberries (both low and high bush). Every effort was made to preserve the fruit for use later in the year. Some berries were dried whole; others were dried and then pulverized. Boiling was sometimes used, particularly with raspberries. It was also this time of the year that

[1]Before the Indians had iron kettles, hot rocks were dropped into the sap.

ducks and geese became quite helpless during a period of moulting and young birds were taken just before they were large enough to fly. Unsportsmanlike? Not when you're talking about food for survival!

September brought the wild rice harvest and another occasion to feast and celebrate. It was perhaps even a greater time for reunions and socializing than the sugar camps. Most harvesting was done by the women, usually two to a canoe. While one paddled or poled the boat through the rice bed, the other sat in front and pulled the rice over the canoe, beating the heads with a stick - thus dislodging the mature kernels. Since all of the rice in each head did not mature at the same time, the harvesters could cover the same area several times a few days apart.

The kernels were further sparated from the husks by beating or trampling and then the chaff was blown away by throwing the rice into the air on a windy day. The kernels were then parched by the fire.

The same animals that are found in the boundary area today were here centuries ago -plus a few more. The earliest inhabitants found such huge beasts as the wooly mammoth and the giant bison. Buffalo,[1] caribou, and elk were common even after white men first arrived. Most animals, such as moose, were probably more plentiful than today, but others, such as deer, may have been less plentiful. But for all of the animal life, hunting was not always easy. Such primitive weapons as spears and bows and arrows gave wild game a great advantage. Predators and disease probably took a greater toll than the Indians, and severe winters were hard on both the hunter and the hunted.

The Indians were a religious people. They believed in a Supreme Being (the Great Spirit), and they believed in a life after death (happy hunting ground). The Ojibway had a multitude of lesser gods or spirits - usually taken from nature - called "manitou." There were also evil spirits called "wendigo." Religion called for such virtues as patience, truth, and honesty, but curses were called down upon enemies. Superstitions and religious legends were numerous but varied somewhat from village to village. Gods were worshipped in prayers, offerings, chants and dances. The Ojibway were particularly conscientious about offering prayers whenever food was harvested or taken in a hunt. Visions and dreams were generated by fasting and meditation.

"The happy hunting ground" was a place where the Indian was free from his struggle for survival and all the necessities of life wer easily attained. Chief Bemidji described the Indian's "Hell" as a place where the hungry Indian could see hundreds of walleyes through six feet of ice with no way to cut through or a deer was always just going over the second hill as he came over the first, or he was very cold and all the wood was too wet to start a fire.

Medicine men were both priests and healers. When herbs or other medicines did not work they exorcised evil spirits. They practiced the "laying on of hands" to invoke a blessing.

The help of the gods was sought before each serious endeavor, whether it be waging war, hunting or whatever.

Dances often included a religious or other serious purpose and were not performed as mere entertainment.

[1]In the 17th century the buffalo probably came only as far east as Lake of the Woods.

The Ojibway had a religious-cultural hero named "Nanabozho," who created the world for the Indian and taught him about the Great Spirit and religious practices. These practices were called "Midewinin," and they were characterized by secret ceremonies and initiations including a guardian spirit for each and a "totem" spirit for each family group or relation. The Ojibways had about twenty totems with as many as 1,000 members in a totem family. It was taboo for members of the same totem to marry. The totem was symbolized by a bird, animal, reptile, or fish. In addition, each Ojibway carried a medicine bag which contained herbs and items such as shells which represented special powers and protection. The priests were called "Mides."

Polygamy was common with the male taking more than one wife.

Upon death, following a ceremony and appropriate mourning,[1] bodies were sometimes bundled on scaffolds or placed in trees - particularly during the cold time of the year - and buried later. The Ojibway tribe traditionally buried their dead in a sitting position facing west. A long, low house-like shelter was constructed over the grave. Food was placed here along with all the deceased would need in the way of tools and weapons to help him in his journey westward "across the river" to his eternal reward. A carved or drawn symbol of the appropriate totem was often placed outside the shelter.

William Warren, the Ojibway author we have previously quoted, was a self-ordained Christian missionary. He told in his "History of the Ojibway" something about his efforts to convert his people to Christianity. He was surprised that the elders of the tribes often knew the Old Testament stories of the Bible - but identified the heroes with Indian names. This led him to speculate that the Indian people could have been descendants of the "Ten Lost Tribes of Israel!"[2]

Missionaries had great difficulty in converting the Indian peoples. To this day many Indians have held to their traditional beliefs; others have adopted a curious blend of these beliefs and Christianity. However, many were "converted" and these converts often had greater success than the white missionaries in introducing the teachings of Jesus to the Indians. But generally there was great resistance and many missionaries despaired at behavior "degrading and immoral" by their standards. Alcohol arrived almost as soon as the missionaries and made their task even more trying. The nomadic traits of the Indian tribes made it difficult to work with them long enough to have an impact. Father Alneau, the Lake of the Woods martyr, was among those directed to locate the Mandan tribe which supposely stayed for generations in one place and "enjoyed" a more advanced civilization and standard of living.[3] He did not live long enough to find them, but his sponsors, the LaVèrendye, eventually explored the Dakotas.

[1]Periods of mourning were often characterized by much crying and loud wailing.

[2]It is interesting that Ojibway grammar has similarities to Hebrew!

[3]The Mandans are believed to have spent some time in Minnesota before settling in central North Dakota. Some who believe in the authenticity of the Kensington Runestone (not generally accepted by historians) attribute the higher standard of living to association with the Vikings described on the Runestone. They further support this theory by the fact the Mandans sometimes used moat-like waterways to protect their permanent dwellings. According to legend, a fair-skinned people lived among the Mandans prior to the smallpox epidemic of 1782. We are also told that a band of marauding Ojibways, Crees, and Assiniboins came upon a helpless tribe in the Mandan area - either the Mandans or Gros Ventres - at the time of the epidemic and took an enormous scalp from a giant of a man as one of their trophies. Did the thick, bushy scalp belong to a decendant of the Vikings??? This scalp, along with the others taken is believed to have been a carrier of smallpox germs back into the lake region.

We are indebted to William Warren for the following picture of life at La Pointe[1] - on Madeline Island at the mouth of Chequamegon Bay on Lake Superior - before guns and powder were common:

> *"Every stream which emptied into the lake, abounded in beaver, otter, and muskrat, and the fish which swam in its clear water could not be surpassed in quality or quantity in any other spot on earth. They manufactured their nets of the inner bark of the bass and cedar trees, and from the fibres of the nettle. They made thin knives from the rib of bones of the moose and buffalo. And a stone tied to the end of a stick, with which they broke branches and sticks, answered them the purpose of an axe. From the thighbone of a muskrat they ground their awls, and fire was obtained by the friction of two dry sticks. Bows of hard wood, or bone, sharp stone-headed arrows, and spear points made also of bone, formed their implements of war and hunting. With ingeniously made traps and dead-falls, they caught the wily beaver, whose flesh was their most dainty food, and whose skins made them warm blankets. To catch the moose and larger animals, they built long and gradually narrowing inclosures of branches, where they would first drive and then kill them, one after another, with their barbed arrows. They also cought them in nooses made of rough hide and hung from a strong bent tree, over the road that these animals commonly traveled to feed, or find water. Bear they caught in deadfalls, which were so unfailing that they have been retained to this day. . ."[2]*

But even in the midst of all this abundance, life could be hard. Cold winter months with heavy snows sometimes made hunting and trapping extremely difficult, and starvation was a familiar enemy. Diseases sometimes came close to wiping out entire species of animals. There were years when the Indians depended almost entirely on rabbits and fish for survival.

In addition to food, the forests of our "Canoe Country" provided fuel, shelter, and material for the construction of boats. The valuable birch tree yielded its pliable bark for covering canoes and lodges and the pine provided pitch with which to seal the cracks and mend the breaks. The forest also gave the Indian his principle luxury -tobacco. The woodlands Indians used the ground inner bark of the Kinikinic (red willow), blended with powdered leaves and roots of other plants. The smoking of the peace pipe was traditional on ceremonial occasions but tobacco was also smoked for pleasure.

The boundary waters themselves made the area a scenic place in which to live and provided relatively easy transportation. The Indian people traveled much more than one would first imagine. For example, John Tanner, the legendary "white-Indian" of Lake of the Woods fame, was kidnapped from his missionary parents on the Kentucky shores of the Ohio River and journeyed as a child with an Ottawa Indian woman who adopted him at least as far west as Saskatchewan. Indians from central Minnesota went as far as Fort Mackinac to trade during the time when white men were frightened

---

[1]La Pointe became the unofficial capital of the Ojibway nation after the tribes moved west from their Sault Ste. Marie headquarters after 1680. Eventually La Pointe had a population of about 1000. After 1770, when the Ojibway had made northern Minnesota safe enough for establishing villages, La Pointe diminished in size and importance. William Warren writes of another reason for the eventual evacuation of the village following that time - cannibalism! It was not brought about by starvation, but by Satanic practices originated by some of the medicine men. As the practice grew, the only answer was to flee.

[2]Warren, William, History of the Ojibway, Minn. Historical Collection, Vol. 5.

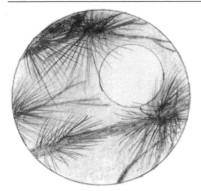

away by the Sioux-Algonquin wars. Others went to Hudson Bay to visit trading posts there in the days before competition from the Northwest Co. forced the H.B.C. to establish posts among the Indians farther to the south. The border waterways also provided contact with other Indians on the move; it was the best east-west route available for crossing the continent and was part of a direct route between the Gulf of St. Lawrence and the Columbia River.

It isn't hard to picture the "Canoe Country" as it might have been prior to De Noyon's adventure. We can imagine Indian villages along the shores and on the larger islands. It is thrilling to think of scores of birchbark canoes gliding over clear waters with towering pine, cedar, spruce, aspen, and birch as background. Late summer blueberry picking and September wild rice harvests must have been spectacular tribal happenings. Romanticists could write many a story of the courtship of the Indian maiden by the young brave in an evening setting with the full moon rising over a rocky cliff and the beams filtering through the pines to the waters below, with the haunting cries of a loon for musical background.

Even when we think more realistically of the fight for survival against the long, cold winters with ice as much as three feet thick and snow drifts waist deep, we can't help but feel the Indians' chances here were a least better than average. The wilderness was hard, the wilderness was cruel; but the odds for survival in this canoe country between Lake Superior and the Lake of the Woods were surely better than in most parts of the North.

CHAPTER TWO
Explorers, Missionaries, Trappers and Traders- The First Whites

What was a twenty-year old Frenchman (De Noyon) doing in our wilderness area nearly a thousand miles from the relative luxuries of eastern Canada in 1688?

What motivated Du Luth - nearly twenty years earlier - to brave the treacherous waters of the Great Lakes and "invade" the land of the Sioux, leading his relatively tiny band of men even into the very "streets" of the legendary village of Kathio[1] on Mille Lacs Lake - the unofficial capital of the Sioux Nation?

Why did Raddison, rejected by his native France, persist until he had the support of the British Crown to form the Hudson's Bay Co., and then explored thousands of miles of wilderness from Hudson Bay on the north to the upper Midwest of present day United States on the south - even before Duluth?

For what reason did Pierre LaVèrendye, in the next century, build his string of seven forts from Rainy Lake to Athabasca?

Was it for adventure? The yearning to explore? For fame? To claim land for their government? Perhaps all of these - but mostly the reasons were economic. It was the desire for wealth, the same economic motivation that makes our free enterprise system work today.

Even in the late 1600's, the waterways of eastern North America were being trapped out. The merchants of Montreal and other eastern cities needed new sources of animal furs with which to supply the lucrative European markets. We know from the journals of people like LaVèrendye that if the traders had their "druthers" they would have spent their time exploring rather than negotiating with Indians for furs, but their expeditions had to turn a profit. Although governments demonstrated spuratic interest in funding explorations in Colonial times, it was the merchants of that day who were willing to finance those ventures which promised a return on their investment. But as soon as the traders spent too much time exploring to the neglect of fur trading, the merchants withdrew their support. As we shall see later in this chapter, LaVèrendye was constantly in difficulty with his sponsors in Montreal and returned east several times to assure continued backing.

In addition to the profit motive, nearly every early explorer of our continent was inspired by the dream of finding a northwest passage to the Pacific and the Orient. Indian guides spoke of large bodies of water to the west and each time an explorer came upon

[1]The Indian name was actually "Izatys," but it was incorrectly copied from Duluth's notes as "Kathio."

an expanse he could not see across, his heart must have pounded with anticipation that it could be the ocean itself. But one cannot overstate the importance of furs to the colonial economy and as the prime motivator in bringing the first white men to our **Canoe Country.**

Although a number of explorers, trappers, traders, and missionaries visited the boundry region between the time of De Noyon's operations (1688) and the arrival of the LaVèrendye party in 1731, few such visits are recorded.

We do know, however, that in 1717, the trader **De la Noue**, built a post at the mouth of the Kaministikwia River on Lake Superior, and, following the footsteps of De Noyon, penetrated to Rainy Lake, where he also established a fort.

Five years later the explorer **Pachot** made the first known chart of the Pigeon River and followed this more southerly water route west to the Lake of the Woods. This southern way then became the better known and most favored route followed by subsequent travelers until about 1800.

Pierre LaVèrendye

Few explorers of this continent have made as significant a contribution as this French Canadian, Pierre Gautherier De LaVèrendye. Born in 1685 in Three Rivers, Quebec - the launching pad for most explorations of that day - he was the son of a governor of the area and his mother was the daughter of a former governor - Pierre Boucher.

LaVèrendye and his sons constructed seven forts, opened the wilderness to fur trading as far west as the Red River and Lake Winnipeg, and explored south into the Dakotas and west perhaps as far as the foothills of the Rocky Mountains.

We are also indebted to him for his disciplined record keeping which gives us keen insight into the hardships and adventures faced by the explorers and traders of that day. He has also provided us with an understanding of the Indian peoples of his time - before the coming of the white man. The records of both the Church of France and the Order of the Jesuits bear witness to the authenticity of LaVèrendye's journals. Letters from Father Jean Pierre Alneau (a missionary hero of these days of exploration) to his mother and sisters in France, which were kept in the family for generations,[1] also collaborate the explorer's diaries.

In an age when travel was often a hardship and always time consuming, LaVèrendye saw a lot of the world. He joined the army at the age of twelve! He fought the British in Boston and the men of the Duke of Marlborough in Flanders. He suffered nine wounds and was left for dead on that foreign battlefield. On his return to Canada he was named Commander of a small trading post on the St. Maurice River. By 1729 he had earned a more important post on Lake Nipigon (Ontario). Not far from Nipigon was Fort Kaministikwia (the actual Fort William), beyond which not much of the West was known.

No doubt the Indians and trappers who came to the fort on Lake Nipigon found an eager listener in its commandant. One such visitor, an Indian - "Anchgoh" by name -told LaVèrendye about the Lake of the Woods and a still larger body of water farther

---

[1]In 1899, a descendant of the Alneau family gave a packet of letters [already 150 years old] to three Jesuit Priests who had come to Vendre, France in that year. The packet had been passed down from generation to generation and included not only Father Alneau's letters to his family and fellow priests but also letters from Jesuits in North American to the martyr's mother after his death.

west. So excited was LaVèrendye that on three successive nights he dreamed that he discovered "the great sea of the West." Anchgoh scratched a map of his travels on birchbark (copies of which may still be seen in the French archives) and LaVèrendye sent this along with a proposal to explore the region to Beauharnois - the Governor of Canada.

In 1730, LaVèrendye responded to an invitation from Beauharnois to meet with him and the colony's engineer, Chauusegros de Lery, in Quebec. Following this conference, a report was prepared for the Minister of Colonies in France and dispatched along with an encouraging recommendation from the Colonial authorities. It was fortunate for LaVèrendye that communications were slow. By the time the negative reply arrived, LaVèrendye had persuaded the Governor to authorize him to (1) solicit financial support from Montreal merchants, (2) construct three forts at Rainy Lake, Lake of the Woods, and Lake Winnipeg, and (3) trade for furs with the Indians as partial compensation for his explorations. LaVèrendye was already on his way when the reply came from Paris saying it would allocate no funds for the endeavor.

LaVèrendye apparently had much less difficulty enlisting the support of the Montreal merchants than the French government. They were starting to feel the competition of the British as a result of Indians traveling north to Hudson Bay with their furs. It is also likely that even at this early date the animals were being "trapped out" along the eastern waterways.

The LaVèrendye party left Montreal June 5, 1731. Although he had a crew of fifty men, it was quite a family affair. Included were three of LaVèrendye's sons: Jean Baptiste, Pierre, and Francois, and a nephew, Christophe Dufrost de La Jemeraye. They passed through Lachine and traveled down the Ottawa. When they reached Fort Machilimackinac, they picked up a Jesuit missionary who was familiar with the country, Father Mesaiger; this completed the authorized contingent of fifty men. One cannot overstate the contributions of these men of God in the exploration and eventual settlement of the Americas.

The next stop was Kaministikwia (Fort William); in twelve weeks they had traveled a thousand miles. On August 6th they arrived at Grand Portage, - after traveling westward along the north shore of Lake Superior. "Grand Portage" meant a rugged nine mile clumb up a rise of 650 feet from Lake Superior to the Pigeon River. Because of the lateness of the season and the rugged country ahead, most of the men opposed going farther.[1] After serious deliberation, LaVèrendye agreed to return to Fort Kaministikwia on Lake Superior with the bulk of his crew. A smaller group - perhaps volunteers - agreed to go on under the leadership of the nephew, La Jemeraye. Jean Baptiste, the oldest son, accompanied the smaller group. This advance contingent was able to reach Rainy Lake without incident and built a fort at the outlet of that lake before winter set in. It is believed that the structure was located on Pither's Point at the source of the Rainy River. The fort was named Fort St. Pierre, in honor of Pierre LaVèrendye.

In the spring of 1732, La Jemeraye returned to his uncle with a glowing report and canoes filled with furs. It is easy to imagine the ecstacy which must have filled the anxious heart of LaVèrendye after the long winter of waiting. Although the reunion at

[1] Their opposition bordered on muting.

Grand Portage took place on May 29, the party did not arrive at Fort St. Pierre until July 14. A smaller party, meanwhile, had headed east after the reunion, bringing the canoes of furs back to Montreal to gladden the hearts of the merchant sponsors of the expedition. We are told that "a large gathering of Indians" met LaVèrendye upon his arrival at the Rainy River fort (St. Pierre). After considerable speechmaking and the exchanging of gifts, the adventurers, accompanied by about fifty Indian canoes, continued westward up the Rainy River to the Lake of the Woods. It must have been quite a spectacle.

After crossing Big Traverse, the party explored the inlets and islands of what is now the Northwest Angle, and finally selected a site on the mainland for the construction of the second fort. It was named "Fort St. Charles" - perhaps in honor of both the Priest, Father Charles Measiger, and Charles de Beauharnois, the Governor of Canada. Many years later, after the fort had disappeared in decay, the dams at Kenora raised the level of Lake of the Woods by nine feet, thus making the site of the fort an island (known today as Magnuson's Island).

In the spring of 1773, La Jemeraye (appointed second in command by his uncle) led a crew back east to report on the success of the mission. He took with him maps of their discoveries and furs collected over the winter. Father Measiger had been in ill health for some time and chose to return east with the party.

The years of 1733 and '34 were years of tension in the Lake of the Woods - Rainy Lake area. A raiding party of Dakota - Sioux had killed four Cree and this tribe and their allies were determined to gain revenge. LaVèrendye's efforts to maintain peace (so that he could continue his trading and exploring) succeeded only in delaying the action for a few months. In the spring of 1734 a small army of nearly 700 braves headed south to raid Sioux villages, probably on the Red Lakes. LaVèrendye's eldest son, Jean Baptiste, accompanied them; it was a price he had to pay in return for the Indians' promise to delay their revenge until spring (LaVèrendye had hoped that by that time tempers would have cooled and plans for retaliation would have been abandoned).

The reconstructed Fort St. Charles   Courtesy Minnesota Historical Society

This proved to be the prelude to all out war between the Dakota-Sioux of Minnesota and the Ojibway - Assiniboin - Cree Alliance of the border region and Wisconsin - a feud that was to last over 100 years, almost up to the time of the Civil War.

Late that spring, LaVèrendye decided the time had come for him to return east and report first-hand these latest developments. No doubt he hoped to solicit further financial support from the merchants of Montreal and possibly even win some contribution from the French government. Before leaving, he instructed one of his men, a man named Cartier, to take a contingent west to Lake Winnipeg and build the third fort at the mouth of the Red River. Tradition has located the site as a few miles below Selkirk on the banks of the Red River. It was later moved to the north bank of the Winnipeg River. Once constructed, the fort was named Maurepas, for the French Colonial Minister.

On his way east, LaVèrendye met his nephew returning to Fort St. Charles. He gave him authorization to replace his son as commandant; Jean Baptiste, in turn, was to join the crew in the process of constructing the new fort.

LaVèrendye seemed always to have been in financial difficulty. This time he was unable to completely regain the faith of the Montreal merchants. However, a compromise was reached and the merchants agreed to finance his work, providing he turned the three forts over to them and they could send some men along to look out for their financial interests. From the point of view of the historian, this was not all bad; it gave LaVèrendye more time to explore.

When he returned to Lake of the Woods in the summer of 1735, he brought with him his youngest son, Louis-Joseph, who had been studying mathematics and map making in Quebec. He also brought with him a new priest, Father Jean Pierre Alneau, for whom the largest peninsula in Sabaskong Bay is named today. The young priest (thirty years of age at this point) had arrived from France only the year before. He had actually finished his seminary training in Quebec. Young Alneau was one of seven recruited by New World Bishop Dosquit from his homeland. He left behind a wealthy, widowed mother and sailed with a premonition he would never see her again. Surviving the voyage to the new world was an achievement in itself. Twenty died during the eighty-day journey - (credited by some as a record for the *longest* time to cross the Atlantic by commercial vessel). Storms, disease, and a plague of lice were very nearly too much.

We know from his letters that Father Alneau was a very devout man who really loved his God. He was not an adventurer; he was a missionary. In Quebec he met and talked with every priest who returned from the frontier post that winter; concerning them he wrote,

> "*. . .the striking example they have given me of zeal, recollectedness, self-denial and interior union with God has, through our Lord's mercy awakened in my heart a true sincere desire to make every effort I can to imitate them.*"

One of the reasons Father Alneau was chosen for this particular assignment was so that he could learn the Indian dialects that he might teach them in their own tongue. We know that he learned quickly, and within a few months was doing just that. We also know that most of the French explorers and voyageurs also learned the Indian languages; this is another important reason for the usually good relations between the French and Indians.

With the passing of another winter, two of LaVèrendye's sons who had had spent the cold months at Lake Winnipeg returned with the news that La Jemeraye was no more. LaVèrendye's able nephew thus became the first recorded white man to die in the West. Although LaVèrendye marked the burial place on a map, the chart has been lost and the exact location of his grave is uncertain. Some historians say it is at the mouth of the Red River, others believe it is where the Roseau River runs into the Red River.

The summer of 1736 was a difficult one at Fort St. Charles. The wild rice had been flooded out the year before; they were generally short of provisions; the supply of gunpowder was dangerously low; and the Sioux were known to again be active on the lake and "looking for scalps." Expected provisions from the East had not arrived. The situation was so serious that LaVèrendye called a meeting of his men (still about fifty in number), and the decision was made to send a small party back to Mackinac Island for relief. This would also mean "fewer mouths to feed" at the fort.

The Massacre

Once the decision had been made the only question was who would go and how many. Father Alneau decided to take advantage of this opportunity to report to his superiors. Perhaps he felt the need for counsel and encouragement. During the long, lean winter he had written,

> *"As for the Indians who dwell here, I do not believe, unless it is by a miracle, that they can ever be persuaded to embrace the faith; for even not taking into account the fact that they have no fixed abode, and that they wander about the forests in isolated bands, they are superstitious and morally degraded to a degree beyond conception. In addition both the English and the French, by their accursed avarice, have given them a taste for brandy and this traffic in liquor with the Indians has brought about the destruction of several flourishing missions, and has induced many an Indian to cast away every semblance of religion. This practice constitutes one of the greatest crosses the missionaries have to endure here among the Indians."*

It was Father Alneau who requested that LaVèrendye designate his oldest son Jean Baptiste, to lead the party. It was decided that nineteen others be added to complete the crew. LaVèrendye said in his personal journal that he chose the best. Many, or possibly all, were soldiers of France. If not soldiers, then voyageurs.

The party left St. Charles the afternoon of June 5, 1736. Tradition holds that they chose an island for camp the first night out - about 18 miles from St. Charles.[1] There's no positive evidence that the place we now call "Massacre Island" was indeed this campsite, but Indian tradition marks it as an island of taboo.

At any rate, the first campsite was the last. A band of Dakota-Sioux fell upon the expedition and killed them all! Some Indians were killed in the fighting. No Indian bodies were found on the island, but some hastily buried remains and bloody canoes were found shortly after the massacre on sand beaches on another part of the lake (Muskeg Bay).

LaVèrendye became more worried when seven days after the party's departure, two Indians arrived at Fort St. Charles and told how one of LaVèrendye's men, Bourassa (not one of the twenty-one), had almost met death at the hands of the Sioux. This was

[1]LaVèrendye said "Seven Leagues".

confirmed in a letter received two days later from Bourassa himself. He was apparently about to be burned at the stake when an old Indian woman intervened. She had been befriended by the French.

A few days later, the long-expected party from Montreal arrived at St. Charles. When they reported that they had not met the three canoes heading east, LaVérendye dispatched a search team with instructions to follow the same route. They returned on the 22nd with the tragic news. They had found the bodies of the nineteen murdered crewmen arranged in a circle, and the remains of young LaVérendye and Father Alneau were in the center of the circle. They reported to the fort that -

> *"the heads had been placed on beaver robes, most of them scalped. Father Alneau had one knee upon the ground, an arrow in his side, his head split open, his left hand against the ground, his right hand raised. The Sieur de LaVérendye was lying on his face, his back all scored with knife cuts, a stake thrust into his side, headless, his body ornamented with the leggings and armpeices of porcupine."*

Later in the summer, a group of Indians from the Sault St. Marie area (Chippewa) who were friendly to the French, came upon the island and piled bolders over the remains of the two leaders. Because of the period of great tension which followed (the Chippewa were begging LaVérendye to lead them in a war of revenge against the Sioux) the bodies were not retrieved until September. LaVérendye wrote in his journal,

> *"On September 17th I dispatched the Sergeant with six men to go and raise the bodies of Rev. Father Alneau and my son and on the 18th I had them buried in the chapel, together with the heads of the Frenchmen killed, which they also brought in accordance to my orders."*

It was the discovery of these buried skulls and skeletons in 1908 by the St. Boniface (Manitoba) Historical Society that verified beyond the shadow of a doubt the location of Fort St. Charles.

LaVérendye had not had an easy life, and this tragic blow of losing his eldest son, his missionary, and nineteen of his best, would have destroyed lesser men. But LaVérendye would not give up, even though conditions in and around the fort grew worse. The Sioux, flush with victory, were boasting they would drive all the white men out of the country. The Crees, Ojibway, and the Monsonis, truly friendly Indians, became so taken up with fighting the Sioux that there was little time for trapping and trading furs. LaVérendye relations with the Montreal merchants were deteriorating, finally forcing him to return east. In the summer of 1737, he set out with fourteen canoes, loaded with furs. He was successful in enlisting support for another expedition but not without considerable difficulty.

Meanwhile, his sons had remained in the West at different forts. However, on August 31, 1738, they all met once again at Fort St. Charles. After doing his best to make sure that his three forts were in capable hands, LaVérendye embarked on an historic exploration of the area farther west. He traveled the territories of the Assiniboine, the Saskatchewan, and the Mandans. He did not get as far as the mountains but saw a good deal of the western plains. Some sources credit him with getting as far as the Black Hills and the Big Horns. A new fort (Fort La Reine) was established on the Assiniboine, the location of present-day Portage La Prairie. This became the new center of trading, replacing Fort St. Charles as the principal fort. LaVèrendye's son, Pierre, was left in command of Fort St. Charles, but there is no record of how long he remained there. In fact, it is not known how long the fort remained in use. No doubt it was retained as a stopping place for a number of years on the route to the forts farther west. We know that LaVèrendye's sons moved west with the activity and *may* have explored as far as the Rocky Mountains. LaVèrendye, himself, returned once more to Montreal, in 1743. Here, he spent several years defending his name against merchants, government officials and jealous colleagues. Once again, he won the battle and was reappointed "Commander of the Western Forts." He was again organizing an expedition when he died unexpectedly on December 5, 1749, at the age of sixty-four.

Pierre LaVèrendye was among the greatest of the French explorers. He and his sons made a major contribution to the opening of the West. When he began his work, Lake of the Woods and everything west were legend. Fifteen years later, the main water routes had been discovered, explored, and mapped, including Lake of the Woods, Lake Winnipeg, Lake Dauphin, Lake Winnipegosis, Lake Manitoba and the Saskatchewan River. Pierre Gaultier de LaVèrendye was a true giant of the North.

We have taken a great deal of time and space to describe the adventures of Pierre-LaVèrendye, partly because few explorers of this continent have made as significant contributions, but also because the excellent documentation gives us keen insight into the challenges and hardships encountered by the explorers and missionaries of our *Canoe Country*. Those who followed were really more traders and merchants than explorers, but they, too, had important roles to play in the development and exploration of the border region. Canoe traffic on these waterways in the years following LaVèrendye varied all the way from "nil" to times when it must have seemed almost congested. In addition to the scores of explorers and missionaries who came this way, there were sometimes over 1000 voyageurs using the waterways - not to mention the several thousands of Indians who lived in the area at that time. But we shall introduce you to only the more famous, or those whose documentation of their work survives. The Hudson's Bay Company required (and did an excellent job of preserving) daily records at each of its outposts. Thus, names associated with that company live on. The Northwest company records, in contrast, have for the most part disappeared.

One cannot help but be impressed by the remarkable experiential backgrounds brought to this country by many of these men - most were well educated; many came from wealthy families; some were titled; others were of high military rank; and still others were physicians, engineers, and scientists. These are the men we will identify, with apologies to the hundreds and perhaps thousands of their associates and subordinates who also passed this way in the first century after LaVèrendye, but are not known to us.

Bourassa (and other Frenchmen)

A contemporary of LaVèrendye and the same man mentioned in his journals; he is credited with building a fort at the mouth of the Vermilion River, at or near Crane Lake. The remains of a fort have also been found on the northwest side of the lake. This closely matches the site of a fort shown on a chart preserved in the archive of France.

According to Grace Nute, author of "Rainy River Country"[1],

[1] Grace Lee Nute, **Rainy River Country,** M. H. S., 1950

"The remains of another French post were found in 1792 in the English River country, north of Rainy River, by James Sutherland, a Hudson's Bay Company man. This old fort was erected on one of the "back roads" from Rainy Lake to the Winnipeg River by a French trader named Burdigno, according to an old Indian woman at Grand Portage in the 1790's, who remembered it as having been built sixty years earlier. It was on Ball Lake, near Sutherland's Escabitchewan House. Probably there were still other posts."

Other Frenchmen followed - including thousands of colorful voyageurs, to whom we will dedicate our next chapter. Among the French traders were Nicolas Joseph de **Noyelles,** Jackques Legardeur sier de **St. Pierre,** and Louis Francois de **la Corne** - all who served as commandants of Fort St. Charles on Lake of the Woods following LaVèrendye and all who knew well the waters, of our **Canoe Country.**

Hudson's Bay Company

INCORPORATED 2ND MAY 1670

Hudson's Bay Co. Influence

Although the French were the first white men in the border country and pretty much dominated the area for a hundred years or more, their influence was to be brought to an end by wars fought on distant battle fields (both on and off this continent) where the French and their Indian allies lost to the British (French and Indian War). The treaty ending the war, and signed in Paris in 1763, gave this part of North America to the English. There had been a diminishing of activity along the border waterways just prior to this time and a few British traders took advantage of the void, even prior to the signing of the treaty. But they too left and, so far as we know, there were no whites in the border region just after 1763. The few who tried to enter were plundered and rebuffed by the Indians. The English were slow to exploit their new territories, but the Hudson's Bay Company was feeling the competition from the Northwest Company in the 1770's and began establishing posts south of Hudson Bay. The Company showed an interest in the Rainy Lake region as early as 1770, but it was not until 1793 that a post was established on the Rainy River. However, LaVèrendye in his journals tells us that the mammouth trading company did have some effect on this area even in his day and that he found the Indians had in their possession firearms and other weapons as well as miscellaneous metal utensils which had been acquired in trading with the Hudson's Bay Company northern posts - perhaps as far north as Hudson Bay itself.

At the outset, the company operated several posts on the southwest shores of the Bay. The Indians brought their furs to these posts and travel by the English traders was unnecessary. But, as the supply of furs was reduced in that area and as the French continued to develop trade with the Indians in the area south of Hudson Bay, the British were finally forced to penetrate the wilderness. The French had been in the area since the 1600's and as the Hudson's Bay operators moved in, conflict was inevitable.

One of the first, if not the first, Hudson's Bay Posts on the **Boundary Waters** was constructed on the Rainy River at Manitou Falls in 1793 by **John McKay.** This preceeded by only one year a post developed for the company by **Thomas Norn** in 1794 at the mouth of the Rainy River. The post at Kenora (Rat Portage) was not developed until 1836, but eventually became the most important Hudson's Bay operation on the Lake of the Woods. The post on the Northwest Angle also came later.

The trappers who did not work for the Hudson's Bay Co. found (here as elsewhere in Canada) that they were no match for the well-financed English company, so they merged themselves into a competitive organization known as the North West Company. The fur trade industry was highly profitable, which only added "fuel to the fire." The area between Lake Superior and the Red River became one of the major scenes of the bloody rivalry. Even the Indians were drawn into the conflict. The rivalry grew so intense and expensive that the two big fur trading organizations finally merged in 1821 into a combination known thereafter as "The Hudson's Bay Company." Following the merger, York Factory on Hudson Bay replaced Montreal as the fur capitol of North America.

In 1869-70 the Company relinquished to the Canadian Government much of the authority granted in its original charter of 1670. In return it received 300,000 pounds and fifteen million acres of land which was to be selected in various parts of Canada.

The Lake of the Woods, Rainy Lake and the rest of our **Canoe Country** were included in the district known as "Lac La Pluie," meaning "Lake of Rain." The following lands were chosen as a part of the settlement and were listed in the annual report of the Hudson's Bay Company in 1872-

Fort Alexander	500 acres
Fort Frances	500 acres
Eagles Nest	20 acres
Big Island	20 acres
Lac du Bonnet	20 acres
Lake of the Woods	50 acres
Whitefish	20 acres
English River	20 acres
Hungry Hall	20 acres
Front Lake	20 acres
Rat Portage	20 acres
Shoal Lake	20 acres
Clear Water Lake	20 acres
Sandy Point	20 acres

Of all these trading posts, only the one at Lac du Bonnet remains in operation (under the Northern Stores Division of H B C) and so far as it could be determined in contacts with the Company, no property has been retained by the company at any of the other sites.

Although little is known today about many of the posts listed, the Hudson's Bay Company provided the following information regarding the location of the posts:

The Eagles Nest Post was located on Eagle Lake about 75 miles east of Kenora; it was opened in 1860 and closed about twenty years later.

The Big Island (Lake of the Woods) operation was small; it opened in 1865 but no closing date information is available.

Lac du Bonnet, the post which remains in operation, is located on the Winnipeg River near the present townsite of the same name.

The post described as "Lake of the Woods" was apparently a small operation on the west side of the lake but other than that no details are available.

"Whitefish" probably refers to an operation on Whitefish Bay of Lake of the Woods.

Shoal Lake was the site of an apparently small and shortlived operation.

Clear Water Lake House was a small post located on what is now called Teggau Lake.

Hungry Hall, near the mouth of the Rainy River.

Fort Frances, at the site of the present city by that name on the Rainy River.

Fort Alexander, at the site of the former North West Company post near the mouth of the Winnepeg River (south bank).

Rat Portage, present day Kenora and Keewatin.

The following documents furnished by the Company give us considerable insight into life at these outposts, the conflict between H B C and the North West Company and the general impact of the huge trading company on **Border Water** history:

At the Source of the Rainy River (Fort Frances)

"As early as 1777 the Hudson's Bay Company was anxious to establish a post on Rainy Lake, but at that time the area was not known to Company employees. It was not until the summer of 1791 that Donald MacKay on one of his inland journeys marked a site for a fort on Rainy River, not far from the entrance to Rainy Lake.

John McKay arrived at this place in September, 1793, but he considered the site marked by Donald MacKay as being unsuitable, so he eventually built his post just below Manitou Falls on Rainy River about 32 miles from the North West Company Fort (situated near the entrance of Rainy Lake). The H B C post was dismantled in October, 1795, and John McKay went to settle at the mouth of the Rainy River. This post was abandoned in the summer of 1797, and the Company did not return to the Rainy Lake area until 1816.

Donald MacPherson of the H B C in a report dated "Lake la Pluie" May 30, 1818, states that he arrived at Rainy Lake from Fort William on November 5, 1816, and found that the North West Company had handed over their fort to the H B C employees. On the instructions of Lord Selkirk, MacPherson took charge of this post on behalf of the Hudson's Bay Company. (Selkirk had captured the North West Company's headquarters at Fort William and its post at Rainy Lake after hearing of the massacre of Governor Semple and his followers at Seven Oakes, in present-day Winnipeg).

On the union of the Hudson's Bay and North West Companies in 1821, Nicholas Garry,[1] governor of the Hudson's Bay Company, visited a number of posts, and he arrived at Rainy Lake July 27, 1821. The following extract is taken from his diary:

". . .at 2 o'clock we started and after running a Rapid we entered the River of Rainy Lake. . .At a quarter before three we arrived at the Portage de Chaudiere which is about 400 paces

[1]Fort Garry, the predecessor to the city of Winnipeg, was named for this trader. Garry had worked for Hudson's Bay Company in London where he had long served as deputy director.

and is made to avoid a very fine Waterfall. On an Eminence close to the Fall is the
Hudson's Bay Post commanding a most beautiful and picturesque situation. The North
West Post is about a mile higher[2] up the River. The Post of Lac La Pluie or Rainy Lake
before the Union of the two Companies was one of great importance. Here the people
from Montreal came to meet those who arrived from the Athabascan Country and exchange Lading with them receiving the Furs and giving the Goods to trade in return. It will
now become a mere trading Post as the Athapascans will be supplied from York Fort. . ."

*After the union of the two companies it was the Fort belonging to the H B C which
was occupied.*

*On or about February 24, 1830, Governor George Simpson married his cousin
Frances Ramsey Simpson. He took his bride to the Red River Settlement and on the
way passed the post at Rainy Lake. Their arrival is recorded by Chief Factor J.D.
Cameron:*

1830 June 1 "Tuesday arrived about 11 o'clock Governor Simpson accompanied by a
young lovely and accomplished Lady whom he married shortly before he left London. . .
They were all off before 5 o'clock p.m. . . ."

*The Hudson's Bay Company's post was always known as "Lac la Pluie" post until
September 25, 1830, Chief Factor J.D. Cameron recorded the change in his journal
as follows:*

1830 Sept. 25 "Saturday. Fine Weather. This morning at Sunrise the New flag staff was
up, and the new flag hoisted - In the Meantime a flaccon of Spirits was broken & spilled on
the foot of the Staff, and the fort named Fort Frances in honor of Mrs. Simpson's Christian
name. All the Whites gave three Hearty Cheers - and the Indians fired above 300 Shots."

*On October 7, 1874, a fire broke out at Fort Frances and destroyed some of the
buildings which were very old and closely huddled together. The destroyed buildings
were replaced and the post continued as a fur trade post until 1897-98 when, owing
to the opening up of the country around Fort Frances, it was no longer possible to
carry on the fur trade business there and the post was consequently transferred from
the Fur Trade Department to the Saleshop Department. This Saleshop continued to
operate until it was destroyed by fire on February 2, 1903.*

Hudson's Bay Company Outpost at
the Mouth of the Rainy River

*John McKay built the first post in the Rainy River area for the Hudson's Bay Com-
pany in 1793. It was located below Manitou Fall. This post was dismantled in 1795
and McKay went to settle at the mouth of the Rainy River where Thomas Norn had
built a post in 1794. This post was abandoned in 1797 as McKay and his men were
transferred to the Red River area. In August 1793 John Cobb of the Hudson's Bay
Company left Osnaburgh for "Mr. McKay's House" but when he arrived on
September 20 he found that the North West Company had pillaged everthing and
burnt the men's house. He wintered at Ash Falls.*

*The post at the mouth of the Rainy River was again occupied during the winter of
1826-27. So far the name given to this Hudson's Bay Company post at the mouth of
Rainy River has not been mentioned in Company documents. The first reference to it
being called "Hungry Hall" is during the trading season of 1832-33. The following
account is taken from "The Great Lone Land" by W. F. Butler:*

". . .on the 31st of July (1870) we stood away from the Portage du Rat into the Lake of the
Woods. I had added another man to my crew, which now numbered seven hands, the last
accession was a French half-breed, named Morrisseau. . .we were running through a vast

[2]It was actually lower down the river.

expanse of marsh and reeds into the mouth of the Rainy River; the Lake of the Woods was passed, and now before me lay eighty miles of the Rivere-de-la-Pluie. . .About five miles from the mouth of Rainy River there was a small out-station of the Hudson's Bay Company kept by a man named Morrisseau, a brother of my boatman. It was a place so wretched-looking that its name of Hungry Hall seemed well adapted to it."

Captain Hushe, who was attached to Coloned Wolseley's Expedition[1] recorded that he left Fort Frances on August 10, 1870, and on the next day approached the mouth of Rainy River. He continued:

"In the wide reaches of the river the strong westerly wind blowing against the current produced a rough chopping sea, against which we rowed hard for three hours, till we came to a small Hudson's Bay post, two miles from the mouth of the river, where we were glad to stop for breakfast. . .The little post at which we breakfasted is kept by a half-breed named Morrisseau, and is called "Hungry Hall. . ."

George M. Grant, in his book, "Ocean to Ocean" recorded traveling down Rainy River on July 27, 1872, and added:

"Of the seventy-five miles of Rainy River, down which we sailed today, every mile seemed well adapted for cultivation and the dwellings of men. At eleven o'clock the moon rose; at half-past twelve we reached Hungry Hall, a post of the Hudson's Bay Company and a village of wigwams. . ."

In 1886 Hungry Hall consisted of two buildings, a trading shop 20 x 16, 1½ stories high, and a dwelling house of 35 x 17, 1½ story high. Hungry hall was closed during outfit of 1892-93. (An outfit ran from June 1 to May 31)."

(End of quote from Hudson's Bay Company Records.)

Peter Pond and Alexander Henry, the elder

were American explorers who passed this way about 1787. They were among the first whites to appear on the scene following the French and Indian War, after which the British gained possession of this part of the continent from the French. Apparently there had been no white traders or trappers on the **Boundary Waters** for three or four years prior to their arrival. Pond is credited with discovering the Methge Portage which opened up Lake Athabasca to the Traders and Voyageurs.

Alexander Henry, the younger,

was a nephew and name-sake of the earlier explorer. He stopped at the North West Company post on Rainy Lake in 1800, while Peter Grant was the factor, and wrote these impressions:

"There is a good garden, well stocked with vegetables of various kinds - potatoes in particular, which are now eatable."

When the opportunity presented itself, dancing was apparently a favorite activity. The gentlemen danced until daybreak, all very merry."

Hugh Faries

kept a diary at the Rainy Lake North West Company post at the outlet of the lake, where he was commander by 1804. He referred to a competitive fort nearby which was opperated by the XY company - a temporary off-shoot of the North West Company. The companies re-united in 1805. Grace Nute, in her "Rainy River Country," gives this revealing summary of Farie's Journal of that same year:

[1]See Chapter 5

Faries directed not only the main post at the outlet of Rainy Lake, but also wintering houses and subsidiary establishments on neighboring lakes and streams, especially on Basswood Lake, Little Vermilion Lake, Lake of the Woods, and the Winnipeg River. Day after day he records how "old Amelle" was making "lisses," or white cedar frameworks for canoe; how "the men" were shaping snowshoes or dog sleds; how they made traps, or "drank all last night"; how "old Godin and Azure" went down-river to make wooden canoes; how the Athabasca River and the Swan River brigades and other flotillas of canoes from the far West and Northwest arrived and left; how outfits were made and sent to Eagle Lake, Clay Lake, Lake of the Woods, Mille Lacs, and other outlying posts; how runners came and went constantly between these establishments and the main fort, bearing news, letters, provisions, and so forth; how Indian and half-breed "girls" of voyageurs, clerks, and partner alike - including the bourgeois, or company partner, in charge of the district, as well as the diarist - rounded up Indians for the trade, made over a hundred pounds of maple sugar for the fort, netted snowshoes, and "were brought to bed of a fine" half-breed boy or girl; how Indians with such picturesque names as "The Liar," "Big Toad," "Frozen Foot," "Porcupine Tail," "Devil," "Big Rat," and "Young Toad" came and went, brought furs and meat, and took away "credits," or provisions and supplies for which their anticipated winter hunt was pledged; and how the master of this hive of industry watched over his hard-working but childlike engages, gave them patent medicines like "Turlington," or bled them when they were ill, punished and rewarded them, gave them minute instructions for every day's occupation, and directed their contest for furs with the neighboring XY fort, superintended by one Lacombe."

Sir Alexander Mackenzie, the elder,

was a partner in the North West Company - in charge of Fort Chipewyan on Lake Athabasca - the western terminal point for many voyageurs. From here he made an expedition to the Arctic Ocean in 1789, for which achievement the Mackenzie River was given his name. In 1793 this remarkable man pressed across the plains, through the wilderness, and over the mountains to the Pacific, thus becoming the first white man to cross the continent north of Mexico! He then returned to England where he wrote his "Voyages" and was knighted. He came back to Canada in 1802 and became the leading partner in the XY Company. After 1804, when the North West Company and the XY Company were re-united, Mackenzie once more became a partner in the North West Company. Several of his expeditions carried him through our **Canoe Country.**

Alexander Mackenzie, the younger,

was a nephew of Sir Alexander and worked under him in the XY Company. After the merger with the North West Company, he also became a partner in the united company. Most of his work was at the posts along the shores of Lake Superior, but he also served at the fort on Lake Athabasca and was in the boundry waters on several occasions. Lord Selkirk had him arrested as a contributor to the Seven Oaks Massacre, but he was acquited in a trial at York.

John Jacob Astor

founded the American Fur Company in 1808, and made it a viable competitor to the Hudson's Bay Company and the North West Company. After the U.S.-Canadian border was roughly established in this region in 1821, he monopolized the fur trade

[1]Grace Lee Nute, **Rainy River Country,** M. H. S., 1950

south of the Great Lakes and on the American soil of our **Canoe Country.** Shortly after the War of 1812, Astor's men reached such Minnesota lakes as Sandy, Leech, and the Red Lakes. However, it wasn't until 1823 that the American Fur Company had posts on the site of present day International Falls and on Little Vermilion Lake.

In the records of his company, we find the following interesting exerpts from business correspondence:

> *November 31 1821: from Ramsay Crooks to his business associate, John Jacob Astor:*
>
> *"Since the British government has legislated us out of Canada, we shall next year occupy three posts within our lines in the vicinity of Rainy Lake to the Lake of the Woods."*
>
> *December 5, 1821: Crooks to Robert Stuart, the agent at Mackinac:*
>
> *"Morrison will next year establish the Rainy Lake country and carry our trade as near as possible to the border line."*
>
> *1823: from Stuart to Mr. Stone of the Stone, Bostwick Co., which combined with Astor's company in that year:*
>
> *"Stuart complained about the unfair competition from the Hudson's Bay Company which traded whiskey to the Indians forbidden by our government. At each post (say three in number). . .we found it impossible to oppose them successfully."*

Henry Schoolcraft

the famous explorer of the Mississippi, served for a time as the Indian Agent at Sault Ste. Marie. The south shore of the Lake of the Woods and the American side of the **Boundary Waters** were included in his district. On August 9, 1824, he wrote in a report on trading posts in his agency:

> *"Pursuant to instructions, I have determined on the following places where trade may be carried on with the different bands within the limits of this agency. . .number 18 at Rainy Lake. Number 19 at War Road."*

We can be quite certain that the post at the mouth of the Warroad River was established no later than 1822.

Although the American Fur Company became a respectable rival of the merged Hudson's Bay Company, the international boundary prevented the bloodshed that characterized the old rivalries prior to that time. However, the Indians were free to trade on both sides of the boundary and indications are that the American FurCompany usually came out second best. In 1833, the American company agreed to a financial settlement from the Hudson's Bay Company and withdrew from their border posts in this region ($300 annually).

David Thompson

was among the great English explorers associated with our **Boundary Waters.** Born in London, England, he attended Oxford before coming to this continent around 1784. He was at first apprenticed to the Hudson's Bay Company, but went to work for the rival North West Company in 1797. Thompson spent many years in the border country, making a significant contribution as a map maker, basing his work on his knowledge of astronomy and the readings he took establishing latitudes and longitudes. His work carried him to the far west where he discovered the Columbia River in 1807. He returned to **Canoe Country** when he was placed in charge of the British Commission to develop the United States-Canada boundary from the St.

Lawrence River to the Lake of the Woods. He also ventured deeper into Minnesota where he erroneously proclaimed Turtle Lake (near Bemidji) as the source of the Mississippi River. Thompson was a pretty fair artist and provided the illustrations for Bigsby's "The Shoe and Canoe," which gave the world its first view of the B.W.C.A.

Dr. John Bigsby
served with Thompson as a member of the British Commission to establish the U.S.-Canadian border. Bigsby Island on Lake of the Woods bears his name. As assistant secretary to the Commission, he kept and published a diary entitled, "The Shoe and Canoe."

Major Joseph Delafield
was in charge of the American portion of the Joint Boundary Commission established to identify the U.S.-Canadian border as provided in The Treaty of Ghent (1814). His journals were published under the title "The Unfortified Boundary."

Sir George Simpson
visited the **Boundary Waters** nearly fifty times. He was particularly interested in the operations of the Hudson's Bay Company here. The H B C operations on Rainy Lake had always been known as the "Lac la Pluie" post, but the name was changed to "Fort Frances" in honor of Mrs. Simpson when she visited there with her husband in 1830 as a bride of but a few months. Sir George was influential in bringing about the merger of the Hudson's Bay Company and the North West Company in 1821. He was appointed Governor of the northern part of the united company and later served as the General Superintendent. Simpson encouraged exploration and he, himself, crossed the continent and made a trip around the world in 1841-42. Sir George liked to travel in style and his canoe was usually propelled by a select group of voyageurs - making his craft the fastest in the north country. A bagpipe playing musician usually accompanied him. One wonders what the wolves, loons and other members of the wild kingdom thought when they heard the unique tones of this remarkable instrument, and how they may have responded!

Dr. John McLaughlin
the Canadian-born physician-explorer, spent several years in the area sometimes wintering at Little Vermilion Lake. In 1814 he was made a partner in the North West Company and was placed in charge of the Rainy River District. While at the Rainy Lake post, he successfully treated John Tanner,[1] who had been ambushed and nearly killed on his way east. As the only physician in the area he no doubt had ample opportunity to ply his trade. McLaughlin opposed the union with the Hudson's Bay Company but after the merger, accepted a commission as Chief Factor. In 1823 he was placed in charge of the Columbia Department on the west coast. Because of his work and leadership in that area he is known to this day as "the Father of Oregon." In 1824 he took charge of Fort George (Astoria); in 1826 he moved farther north where he constructed Fort Vancouver. In his later years, McLaughlin left the Hudson's Bay Company and started a general store in Oregon City, and there lived out his legendary life.

[1]The "Falcon" - white Indian of Lake of the Woods fame.

Lord Thomas Selkirk

Our **Boundary Waters** were the gateway to the establishment of an experimental colony in the wilderness of North America - a true story as spectacular as fiction. The colony was the dream of British-born Lord Thomas Selkirk - a dream inspired by letters from the brother of an assistant, Miles Macdonell. The brother, John Macdonnell, had passed through the border area as early as 1793, on his way to the prairies of Saskatchewan, and had kept a diary of his experiences. Selkirk wanted to help the disadvantaged of his day and envisioned the American colony as the vehicle.

To make his dream a reality, the English nobleman believed he needed a great deal of land, and since the Hudson's Bay Company was the chief landholder in the area in which he was interested, he engineered the purchase of a controlling share of Hudson's Bay Company stock (at a time when the company was in financial difficulty because of the naval blockades during the Napoleonic wars). The North West Company was well aware of Selkirk's plans and strongly opposed them - first through an unsuccessful effort by Sir Alexander Mackenzie to get control of a large block of Hudson's Bay stock, and later by violence and bloodshed. Meanwhile, Selkirk used his position to arrange the cession to himself of 116,000 square miles of territory, including Rainy Lake, much of the Rainy River basin, Lake of the Woods, and stretching as far west as the Red River of the North. He called his new land "Assiniboia," after the tribe of Sioux Indians living in the area.[1] Settlers soon arrived from the British Isles (and later from Switzerland) and developed a colony near the present site of Winnipeg and St. Boniface, Manitoba. The North West Company answered with a show of force, capturing the Hudson's Bay's posts in the area and destroying the embryonic villages along the Red River, killing twenty or more of the colonists - including the man Selkirk had made Governor, John Semple[2] - and taking others prisoner. It became known as the "Seven Oaks Massacre."

Selkirk struck back by hiring mercenaries from the Napolenic wars - mostly Swiss. He placed a man named Peter Fidler in charge of capturing the first target - the Rainy Lake Post, in the winter of 1816. However, when the North West Company clerk, J.W. Dease, was called on to surrender, he calmly refused. Fidler was not certain he had enough men to storm the fort, so he returned all the way to Fort William for reinforcements and a pair of small cannons. This time, badly outnumbered, Dease gave up the Rainy Lake Post without a fight. Now Selkirk's men were ready to proceed west to attack the Red River forts. Being winter, they felt the need for a guide to show them the shorter routes across land, and so they hired John Tanner - the "white Indian," the "Falcon" from Lake of the Woods - along with about twenty of his braves. Selkirk had placed a Captain D'Orsonnens in charge of this expedition and his aide, Mike Macdonell, also joined the group.

According to Tanner, he chose the traditional Indian route - via the Roseau bogs and river. Fort Daer (at Pembina) gave up without a fight, but Fort Douglas (where the Red and Assiniboine Rivers meet) was no such easy mark. While the mercenaries were

[1]See page 9.

[2]A Leech Lake Ojibway, named Maji-gabo, took "credit" for the slaying and scalping of Governor Simpson.. Schoolcraft once met him and described Maji-gabo as "tall, gaunt, and savage looking."

bickering over the best way of attack, Tanner and his men, augmented by a few of the more venturesome Swiss soldiers, scaled the stockade at night, surprised the defenders, and captured the fort. In appreciation, Lord Selkirk took a deep, personal interest in Tanner and rewarded him with a twenty pound/year stipend for life.

Selkirk was now free to restore his colonies, and he did. These communities eventually developed strong ties with St. Paul and Minneapolis via the Red River ox cart trails. In fact, about 300 of the Swiss settlers grew disillusioned and followed the trails -one way - to Fort Snelling (in the 1820's), carrying their possessions in ox carts and driving their livestock before them. But many remained in Selkirk's colonies and with the coming of first the Dawson Trail, and then the railroad, ties were established with eastern Canada - and the metropolis of Winnipeg was born - something far beyond even the imaginative dreams of Lord Thomas Selkirk.

Peter Grant,

was a partner in charge, for a time, of the Rainy River District of the North West Company. He followed Boyer and Shoults as commander of the Rainy Lake post and spent at least one winter (1805) at the fort on Little Vermilion Lake, thus indicating by his presence (as a partner) that it was indeed important to the operations of the company.

John Cameron,

son of a loyalist who fled to Canada during the American Revolution, at first served with the North West Company and was appointed Chief Factor of the Columbia District under the merger. In 1824 he exchanged positions with Dr. McLaughlin and remained in charge of the Rainy Lake District until 1832.

Major Stephen Long,

represented the United States in determining the location of the 49th parallel in 1823 the boundary between Canada and the United States west of the Lake of the Woods as specified in the Convention of 1818 which followed the War of 1812. He and his party also used the waterways of our *Canoe Country.*

Simon McGillivray,

son of William McGillivray for whom Fort William was named, authored the 1825 Hudson Bay Co. report for the Rainy Lake District. His mother was an Ojibway. McGillivray was privileged to travel in Europe and was highly respected by the leadership of the fur industry of that day.

William Morrison,

was on Rainy Lake in 1825. He originally served with the North West Co. but was picked up by John Astor after the merger. He claimed to have discovered the source of the Mississippi River (Lake Itasca) in 1804 - twenty-eight years before its discovery by Schoolcraft. However, he did not make his claim until after Schoolcraft published his conclusion. Morrison County in Central Minnesota was named for William Morrison and his brother, Allan.

Dr. William Borup,

was a Danish educated physician and fur trader who arrived at the site of International Falls in 1830. He was another example of the excellent "breeding" and education of the traders of that day.

Roderick McKenzie,

succeeded Robert Logan as commander of the Rainy Lake post. In the records of the 1819 - 1820 season, he told of the first mass migration of settlers through the boundary waters, bound for the Red River colonies. They followed the Fort William Kaministikwia River route to Lac La Croix, where it joined the traditional route which originated at Grand Portage and the Pigeon River. Starting about 1802, the northern route was preferred by Canadians because they avoided U.S. soil and the possibility of paying duty on goods they may have been carrying. Hundreds more were to follow via this route, until the railroad reached Kenora in 1881.

Simon Dawson and Henry Hind

In 1857, the Canadian government assigned Dawson, a surveyor-explorer, and Hind, a naturalist, the task of finding the elusive all Canadian route to the Red River colonies. They searched in vain for the old Indian trail via the Warroad River, Hay Creek, and Roseau River - with portages in between. On Lake of the Woods they were surprised to find the Indians engaged in quite a farming operation on Garden Island with several acres under cultivation. When the Indians caught them sampling their crops they scolded them and refused to show them their secret route to the Red River country. Actually, it wouldn't have been of much help anyway because it crossed United States soil.

Although they failed in their primary mission, Hind learned and recorded a great deal about the plant and animal life of the area.

The Hind-Dawson Expedition   Pictured in Harper's Weekly

The canal at Fort Frances   Final Report of the International Joint Commission

Dr. George M. Dawson[1]

was commissioned in 1873 to find an all-Canadian route from Montreal to the Red River and Lake Winnipeg to service the fledgling colonies founded by Lord Selkirk.

In his first effort he discovered the Roseau River route from Lake of the Woods west -the same as used by Tanner in leading Selkirk's Swiss mercenaries in their recapture of Forts Daer and Douglas. This proved unsatisfactory because it crossed American soil.

The ultimate solution was to use the established waterways through our **Canoe Country** from Lake Superior to Lake of the Woods - portages and all - and then carve a road through the wilderness west of the lake to the prairies. Thus, the "Dawson Trail" became a reality, starting where Harrison's Creek flows into the Angle Inlet and ending at Fort Garry (Winnipeg). The route from the Angle west was all by land, first by ox carts and later by stage lines. By 1874, the Dominion Government had spent a million and a quarter dollars (no mean sum for thoses days) on the Dawson route, and in that year more than 300 emigrants followed it to the Red River and Lake Winnipeg area.

The Dominion Government was so determined to break through the wilderness that even a proposal to develop a system of canals from Lake Superior to Lake of the Woods was taken very seriously. At one point the administration proceeded with the the actual construction of a canal at Fort Frances and a large number of men were moved into the area. These became the first permanent settlers in the Fort Frances-International Falls region and along the south shore of Lake of the Woods. However, a change in administration in 1875 resulted in the plan being postponed and then dropped altogether. Had the canal plan succeeded, it would have dramatically changed our **Canoe Country**, but probably not for the better!

Ernest Brown,

was a taxidermist and naturalist from Warren, Minnesota, who traveled the **Boundary Waters** frequently and gave us, through his diaries, a vivid picture of the area at the turn of the century.

Missionaries

frequently accompanied explorers, but were not considered essential by most of the more business-like traders. By 1816, Catholic missionaries began arriving in **Canoe Country**; in that year, **Father Pierre Tabeau** reached Rainy Lake. The Bishop of Quebec had directed him to offer his services to the Red River colonists, but inasmuch as he preferred to work with the North West Company, he stayed on at Rainy Lake.

Two years later, in 1818, other priests arrived who did work their way to the Red River area; they were **Fathers William Edge, Severe Dumoulin, and Joseph Provencher. Dumoulin** is credited with laying the ground work for the establishment of the Rainy River Catholic Mission.

Eventually, emissaries of every major faith (and some not so well known) arrived in this border region. Most came to work with the Indians, but others also served the miners and loggers of later years. So far as we know, **Father Alneau** was the only martyr in this area, but the living conditions were very difficult and the work was often frustrating. Yet, these men of God made their mark and the seeds of Christianity they planted bear

[1]Dr. George M. Dawson (1849-1901); Director, Canadian Geological Society; mapped much of Canada: Dawson City of Yukon Territory was named for him.

fruit to this day.

Fur trade in the Canoe Country has never died. Men and boys still set their traps along these wilderness waterways (where the law allows) for beaver, muskrat, mink, fox, weasel, otter, fisher and lynx. Their forefathers had a little broader selection, including wolves, marten, and wolverine. All three still live in the area, but wolves are protected on United States soil and the other two are scarce. But the importance of fur to the economy waned about the time of the coming of the railroad to Lake of the Woods and Rainy Lake in the 1880's. Agriculture, mining, and logging soon had a far greater impact - but they cannot take away from the glory days when traders, trappers, and voyageurs were the kings of the wilderness!

CHAPTER THREE
The Voyageurs

So great their achievements, so spectacular their endurance, so colorful their attire, so unique their mission - they could have come out of fiction or modern day adventure comic books - but they were very much for real - these voyageurs of our North American wilderness.

In the history of man there has never been a system of trade or transportation quite like it. Few physical accomplishments can match those achieved by the voyageurs; they demanded as much of their bodies as Olympic athletes - and it was no one time venture - it was repeated again and again for more than two hundred years!

When, where, and how did it all begin? It started in the 1600's with the French settlements along the St. Lawrence River. A demand was created in Europe for American furs almost as soon as the colonies became a reality. Man had worn the skins of animals from the beginning, but during the days of the great European empires, furs really came into their own with their practical, durable beauty. Earlier in history they had been reserved in some countries for royalty only; this, of course, added to their prestige and desirability. With the discovery of a seemingly endless supply in North America, the demand for furs simply exploded. Futhermore, the American fur bearing animals were generally larger than their European cousins. The Indians added an exotic touch by wearing furs next to their bodies in winter. These hides went for a premium because the body oils gave the fur a special sheen and body friction softened the pelts.

The St. Lawrence valley was once rich in furs, especially that of the coveted beaver but the supply was quickly depleted by heavy trapping. In order to bring in even more hides from the remote regions, trade fairs were held in places like Quebec and Montreal. However, the fur business became so lucrative some of the more enterprising traders intercepted the Indians on their way east and did their trading out in the wilderness, thus drying up the source of furs for the trade fairs. Competition soon forced exploration of the Great Lakes and the streams that emptied into those great bodies of water and, before long, forts and their auxiliary trading posts were under construction. The French government felt the need to regulate the fur industry and began licensing the traders. As the traders ventured west they needed help - and so they engaged men from the villages along the St. Lawrence River to paddle the canoes and do the many chores; these men were at first called "engagees." Later, they were more appropriately called "voyageurs," which in French simply means "travelers."

It wasn't long before posts were established all along the shores of the Great Lakes.

We saw in the last chapter how Duluth developed an operation on the northwest shore of Lake Superior in 1679. Soon thereafter men like De Noyon penetrated our *Canoe Country*; he reached Lake of the Woods in 1688 or '89. But it was a Yankee, Peter Pond, who was guided by the Indians across the 12 mile Methye Portage to Clearwater River and Lake Athabasca in 1787, thus making it possible (more than one hundred years after the first voyageurs hit the trail) to harvest furs in the area we now call "Saskatchewan" nearly 3000 miles west of Montreal.

Meanwhile, the voyageurs became an institution, with fairly uniform traditions, techniques, skills, and even food and dress. They were also alike in size and general physical appearance. Although strength and endurance were important attributes for the voyageur, size was actually a handicap. There just wasn't room in the canoes for big men - the more human weight the less room for the pay-load. Thus most voyageurs were about five and a half feet tall, or less, and usually of slight build, but wirey.

Those who knew them first-hand have recorded that voyageurs were also very much alike in character and disposition. We are told they were volatile in emotion, fiercely proud of their occupation, eager to meet a physical challenge, loyal, honest, meticulously polite, and basically religious. Their vices (or they would say, "pleasures") were smoking, drinking and occasional gambling. We are led to believe that nearly every voyageur carried a clay pipe and tobacco pouch on his sash. On the more difficult portages or on long stretches of water he was given a smoking break each hour ("poses") - and we read that the cloud of smoke that hung over the portages long after the men had passed on their way was testimony to the enthusiasm with which they enjoyed their repass. In fact, distance was measured in "poses" or by "the pipe" rather than in miles. Drinking, on the other hand, was more carefully regulated by those in charge - and was saved for special occasions or as rewards. High wine was apparently the most common strong drink.

Their dress was as colorful as the voyageurs themselves. In the early years they were clothed much like their Indian friends (from whom they learned so much): moccasins, buckskin leggings, a breechcloth, and bare skin from the waist up. In colder weather they would wear a deerskin jacket of sorts. But in later years, the more practical cloth garments became more common. A blue or red hooded jacket seemed to be a favorite, and nearly everyone wore a gaily colored sash. Neck scarves were also common and a cap of some kind was universal. Most were made of wool and red was the favorite color - with a tassel - usually dropping along side the ear. When their hair grew too long, they might braid it. Sometimes a feather was added to the cap as a special touch; an imported ostrich plume was preferred to those of native birds.

The voyageurs are as well remembered for their singing as for their dress. Never have men sung more lustily at their work. It must have been a very special experience to hear the songs of the voyageurs drifting across the waters through the early morning fog. Most of the chansons were timed to synchronize their brisk paddling; all were designed to lift their spirits - even those that were about long, lost sweethearts and home. Many of the songs had crossed the Atlantic with the French immigrants; others were composed along the St. Lawrence; and still others were spontaneous and original. Many have been preserved to this day - every boy scout knows the swinging melody of "Alouette." A few of the songs were even religious - reminding the voyageurs while car-

The dress was as colorful as the voyageurs themselves

rying canoes or packs along the portage, for example, of Christ carrying his cross. Singing was so important to morale and performance, that a good lead-singer was often given extra pay.

The voyageurs got along well with the Indians and they accepted them as equals. They befriended them, inter-married with them, and counted the braves as brothers. The English, in contrast, generally kept the Indians at arms length and at best developed a paternalistic attitude towards them.

Each spring as the ice went out, about 400 voyageurs (during the peak years) left Montreal and headed west. By tradition, each man stopped at St. Anne's church (their patron saint) to make a contribution to the collection box for the work of the church and to seek a blessing and assure a safe return. The canoes fought the current up the Ottawa River, then the Mattawa to Trout Lake. After a portage into Nipissing, it was "down hill" on the French River to Lake Huron, past Sault Ste. Marie, into Lake Superior, and then west across that great inland sea arriving at Grand Portage about the end of June (about 1800 miles from their point of origin.[1]) Meanwhile, at ice-out, about 700 or more other voyageurs left the posts in the west where they had wintered (some as far as Athabasca country) and worked their way towards Lake of the Woods, where they entered our **Canoe Country** and followed the waterways so familiar to us: Rainy River, Rainy Lake, Namaken, Loon River, Lac la Croix, Crooked Lake, Basswood River, Basswood Lake, Knife Lake, Saganaga, the Granite River, Gunflint Lake, Height of Land, Arrow Lake, Mountain, Moose and the Fowl Lakes, and the Pigeon River to Fort Charlotte, where they took their last portage - all nine miles of it -to Grand Portage itself. It just wasn't possible to make the journey from Montreal to the western forts and return in a single season. That is why there were two distinct groups of voyageurs: the "pork eaters" who carried trade goods from Montreal to Grand Portage and brought back furs on their return trip, and the "hommes du nord" (men of the north) who had arrived from western outposts and would return with the trade goods to exchange with the Indians for furs the next winter.

Now it's easy to understand why the men of the west were called by their several titles: "men of the north," "Nor'Westers," "hivernauts"[2] (winterers), or "coureurs de bois" (wood runners),[3] but why were the Montreal based voyageurs called "pork-eaters?" The answer lies in one of the staples in the voyageurs diet - lyed corn boiled in a can of water, with a couple of spoons of melted pork fat added to difuse the kernels and make a stew the consistence of pudding. It may also be that the term had reference to the fact these men enjoyed domestic meat all winter while the "winterers" in the west lived on wild game.

The "men of the north" generally looked down on the "pork eaters" and their occasional ridicule at Rendezvous sometimes ended in fights. For this reason, their camps were kept separate at Grand Portage.

The annual Redezvous lasted about two weeks and it is a wonder the forts remained in one piece after the revelry. In fact, a jail was maintained for those who became too

[1] There was usually an "R and R" stop at Mackinac while fresh supplies were taken aboard.

[2] Employees of the Hudson's Bay Company.

[3] Usually referred to unlicensed traders.

unruly. In addition to the thousand or more voyageurs, about twice that many Indians were usually on hand to join in the festivities. Of course all the time wasn't spent celebrating. The large packs of trade goods from Montreal had to be opened and repacked in 90 pound canvas-wrapped bales. Furs were sorted, accounted for and again tied in bales for the trip east. Then, too, there were canoe and equipment repairs to be made. Grand Portage was also a canoe factory[1] - with upwards of 70 of the birch-bark vessels being constructed (mostly by the Indians) each season. Rendezvous time also meant payday for the men of the north. The "pork eaters" were generally paid part of their earnings when they left Montreal and the balance upon their return.

When the French chose Grand Portage for a trading post, they chose well. Over the years, all of the major trading companies had posts here: the North West Company, the Hudson's Bay Company, the "XY" Company, and in later years, the American Fur Company. All were relatively large operations, Macdonnell described the North West fort as including sixteen buildings. The gates to the stockades were closed at night and sentries posted - not so much to watch for attack as to be on the lookout for fire.

Located on a bay, the landing beach was sheltered by two points: "Hat" and "Raspberry." A small island, "Mutton" by name, lay at the entrance to the bay. It is the same today as it was then.

Contests of strength and endurance during Rendezvous often had a purpose. The nine mile portage around the rapids and falls of Pigeon River gave ample opportunity for the men to show their prowess. Voyageurs considered this experience as one which separated "the men from the boys." Wagers and challenges characterized the portage. Each man was expected to carry eight - 90 pound bales (usually two at a time). However, as a bonus for anything over that load, they were paid one Spanish dollar per bale. A normal load of two bales at a time meant a total of 72 miles of portage, so the stronger men would try to take more. The record haul was reported to be a wager won by a voyageur who carried 820 pounds (more than nine bales) uphill for one mile! And the portage must have seemed all uphill since the spot where they came out on the Pigeon River is about 650 feet above the level of Lake Superior. Little wonder the only hazzard to health more serious than hernia was drowning.

The voyageurs, though small of stature, must have been remarkable physical specimens. Paddling from pre-dawn to after dark just had to develop tough arm, shoulder, and stomach muscles, and the miles of portage surely made a difference in their legs, backs and necks. Neck muscles? True - the voyageur's neck absorbed some of the strain from the super heavy loads, because a head strap or tumpline (sometimes called a "portage collar") extended from around the forehead down over the shoulders and then the hips, trailing close to the ground. Cradled in the bottom of the tumpline was the first bale - tied in with smaller straps. Additional parcels were placed on top of the first and tied in place. In this manner the stronger voyageur carried as many as three or four of the 90 pound bales at a time. The men kept their balance by leaning forward and trotting at a fast pace. Passengers traveling with the voyageurs recorded that they were hard pressed to keep up, though empty handed.

The longer portages were traversed in stages. After going about a half-mile, the men

[1]Rainy Lake Indians were also well known canoe manufacturers and the trading companies purchased them for use by the Voyageurs and traders.

Using a Tumpline to balance the load

set their loads down and returned to the canoe for the next load. When the canoes were empty they, too, were portaged. The smoke break or "pose" was the incentive that kept them going - it meant the only rest they would have all day except the stop for breakfast. The "pork eaters", with their huge Montreal canoes, had relatively few portages compared to the "men of the north"; they carried the canoes (upside down) with a six man team, two at each end and two in the middle. The smaller north canoes required only four carriers.

If you have ever portaged a canoe over a rocky trail with tangled brush that reached out and entrapped your ankles, with knee deep mud in the low spots, and hoards of insects (mosquitoes, black flies, gnats, and "no-seeums") that knew how to torment you when your hands were occupied - then you have some idea of what these men went through. Remember, too, the birchbark canoes were plenty heavy (500# for the Montreal and 300# for the north), yet extremely fragile.

From two or three to thirty or more canoes traveled together in "brigades."

If the voyageurs ahead of you were from a rival company, it was not beyond them to gleefully drop trees across the path[1] to make your job even more difficult and time consuming. After all, if you couldn't arrive at your destination by freeze-up, you had to go the rest of the way on foot or hope to trade with Indians wherever you ended up - that is if you could find them.

There was little time for frivality on the journey, but there were special occasions. When the Grand Portage was conquered on the return west, and all packs were at Fort Charlotte on the Pigeon River - high wine was traditionally broken out for a celebration. Then, too, if a "pork eater" happened to be along - converting to a Nor'Wester - there was usually an initiation ceremony the first night out. After the hazing, the tenderfoot was expected to supply a round of drinks and take an oath that he would never let any "pork eater" enter the north country without a similar ceremony.

Hopefully, there would be stop-overs at forts along the way for more serious celebrating and even dancing. If there were no women handy (and there seldom were) the men had dances of their own called "rounds" - not unlike those of Greek or Jewish origin - where men simply danced in a circle, sometimes with hands clasped or arms on shoulders, to the tune of a couple of men beating on kettles or whatever else was handy.

But the day to day routine of paddling and portaging was strenuous to say the least. Everything had to move at a brisk pace in order to make the winter forts by freeze-up. Those who traveled with the voyageurs and wrote of their experiences, agreed that the days usually began well before sun-up, often as early as 3 a.m., and normally did not end until well after dark - thus making a 15 to 18 hour day! Only extreme weather disrupted the routine. Paddling was rapid - 40 strokes to the minute and even faster. Portages, as we have said, were covered at a trot. When the going was good they made 60 or even 80 miles a day.

There were only two meals: the first, breakfast, customarily came only after three hours of paddling on empty stomachs; Supper was as late as 10 o'clock at night and eaten only after all daylight had been exhausted. The menu wasn't much to look for-

[1]By 1802, there were so many trees across the trail it is believed to be one reason the British moved their operations to Fort William.

ward to, at least not by our standards. One wonders how it was enough to keep the men going at their torrid pace. Listen to this recipe:

1 qt. lyed corn (or dried peas) (Lye was used to prevent spoiling)
1 gallon water
2 spoons melted suet or bacon fat
Boil for two hours or until it has the consistancy of pudding.

Then there was "rubbaboo" - flour stirred into boiling water to which pemican was added. If there was time or good fortune enough to acquire game or fish enroute - this was also added to the "stew." Pemican was a blend of dehydrated buffalo or moose meat and berries - dried and powdered fine. At one time when buffalo were still plentiful on the prairies, the Sioux and other Indians prepared large quantities of pemican as a trade item. Many a white man developed a taste for it.

Then there was "galette" or unleavened bread - similar to the "bannock" prepared by the voyageurs of today. Water and flour were simply kneaded into a dough. If birds' eggs were handy, they were blended in. Small flat cakes were formed and then fried or baked by the fire - often on a rock.

Of course, if tragedy struck and the provisions were lost, the men had to live off the land or starve. Radisson - before the day of the voyageurs - told of warding off starvation by scraping the lichens off rocks and boiling them in water until they formed a dark, glue-like substance. Don't try it unless you're starving - you won't like it!

The greatest danger to the voyageurs were the rapids. Some were so dangerous the home office in Montreal forbade the men to run them. Yet, most voyageurs preferred to gamble with their lives rather than jog the miserable portages with several hundred pounds on their backs. Crosses marked the graves of those who gambled and lost. It is said that the banks of one of the more dangerous rapids were lined with thirty crosses, even though it was outlawed by the North West Company. The fact that the canoes were so fragile made the rapids even more formidable. Every canoe contained a repair kit consisting of several rolls of birchbark, wattape (twine made from the roots of certain trees like spruce), and cedar strips. If a canoe was destroyed enroute, a new one could usually be constructed from materials found most places in the forest in about four days. If the packs became wet, a halt was called to dry out the contents.

The canoes were a remarkable creation. No nails, just birchbark over cedar strips tied together with wattape and sealed with pitch from the pine tree or gum from the spruce. Thwarts across the top of the canoe held its shape. Seats, if any, were narrow. The canoes used by the voyageurs were basically the same as those used by Indians for centuries - only larger. Whereas the traditional Indian Canoe was fouteen or fifteen feet in length, the north canoe was 25 feet and the Montreal canoes were 35 to 40 feet in length. The latter weighed about 500 pounds and could handle a cargo of from 5000 to 6000 pounds - including the crew of 12. The steersman or "gouvernail" stood in the stern and used a long, wide paddle as a rudder. The captain or "avant de canot" was in the prow. His paddle was the longest of all and was used to ward off rocks while going through rapids. The rest of the crew were called "milieu" or "middlemen"; they were the paddlers who gave the boat momentum. Their paddles were three and one-half to four feet in length and extremely narrow by today's standards - about three inches. The north canoes had the same arrangement but a smaller crew - eight men - and carried about 3000 pounds.

Because of the fragile[1] nature of the canoe, it could not be pulled up on the beach without first emptying the cargo. It was the duty of the "endmen" to jump into waist-deep water and stabilize the boat while the "milieu" did the unloading. Sometimes the canoes were left to float off shore over-night, anchored only with a pole with one end across the gunwhales and the other on shore. If there was bad weather at night, the vessels were emptied of their cargo and over-turned to provide shelter. It was even more difficult to navigate upstream through shallows or rapids than going with the current. If they were deemed to be "not too hazardous," the men would pole the canoe or "track" it by leaving only the steersman aboard while others towed the boat from the shallow waters or from the shore. Even if half of the cargo had to be removed, it was worth the effort rather than portaging everything.

If there ever was a "super-voyageur," it was the Athabascan. Because he traveled so far, his challenge was the greater. Then, too, he had to overcome the 12 mile Methye portage just after leaving Athabasca and its famous Fort Chipewyan. The portage included a 700 ft. cliff which was conquered by using a sled-like contrivance to cradle the canoes. If the ice-out was late, the Athabascans could not make Grand Portage in time for the Rendezvous, and so for a number of years an "Athabascan House" was operated on Rainy Lake as their terminal point.

In the days before the merger, when the Hudson's Bay Company was extending its influence south from Hudson's Bay, the Scots and English used some canoes, but also develped their own kind of boat. They were wooden, double-prowed, over-sized row boats which varied between 28 and 40 feet in length. They were named "York boats" -after York Factory, the Hudson's Bay trading post where they were manufactured. Most of the men who manned them were experienced oarsmen from the Orkney islands off the north coast of Scotland (therefore called Orkneymen). Although clumsy in appearance when compared to the canoes of the Indians and voyageurs, they proved practical and durable on the larger rivers and on open waters. But somehow, the Scots and Englishmen who propelled these York boats lacked the color and romantic flair of the French Canadians with their swift canoes. In each case, the men and their vessels were well matched.

During the winter months when the "pork eaters" were enjoying relative comfort in their homes along the St. Lawrence, the "men of the north" were enduring the rugged wilderness outposts where many of them turned "trader" -meeting the Indians at these outposts and exchanging the goods they had transported the previous summer for their furs. Trade goods included many things: guns, powder, shot, liquors, knives, kettles, other cooking utensils, sewing instruments, flour, salt, grease, trinkets, cloth, items of clothing, and blankets. Most trade items were manufactured abroad: hardware and cloth in England, beads in Italy, wine in France, and rum in the West Indies. The famous Hudson Blanket was a favorite and is still popular on today's market. The quality and size of the blanket was graded in "points." The points, in turn represented

[1]Voyageurs even had to be careful not to move about in the canoe or the gum seals could be broken.

the number of beaver pelts which would be required in trade. Thus, a two point blanket was traded for two beaver skins.

The voyageurs had other winter chores - cutting firewood, hunting, cutting construction timbers, rendering lard from the back fat of animals, and even erecting buildings. Sometimes entire forts had to be constructed. Grace Nute, in her book, "The Voyageurs,"[1] tells us that no nails were used; the logs were grooved and notched to fit tightly together. Chimneys were made of mud mixed with sticks or stones. White clay was available in some areas and used both as a plaster and whitewash. Oiled deerskins substituted for glass in windows, and although one could not see through them, they did admit light. Roofs were often made of thatched bows, but shingles were used on the more permanent buildings. However, the cabins within the stockades were not uncomfortable. Permanent forts had gardens; Indians were employed to supply meat; and hogs were even imported to butcher and eat on very special occasions.

Winter travel was difficult and usually on foot with snowshoes. The more fortunate had dog teams, and were usually supplied with animals from the Indian villages.

Most "men of the north" were married - often to Indian maidens - who impressed them with their small stature, soft skin, and tiny hands and feet. The off-spring of these marriages stayed on in the west to help develop that part of Canada.

The age of the voyageurs lasted almost to the turn of this century. The coming of steamboats, ox carts, stage coaches, and then the railroad made the canoe obsolete. The economy changed, too. Logging and mining were more profitable - particularly as furs went out of fashion in western Europe.

Gone is the Voyageur, but his achievements challenge our imagination and inspire us to stretch our own personal performance in other areas of endeavor. The voyageur showed us that we seldom do more than scratch the surface of our abilities. We are tied in spirit to these vivacious little Frenchmen as we paddle the very same waters and tred the very same portages. What a privilege!

[1]Grace Lee Nute, *The Voyageurs,* Minnesota Historical Society

CHAPTER FOUR
UNTANGLING A BORDER

The Minnesota-Ontario border was established by the Treaty of Paris in 1783 at the conclusion of the American Revolutionary War - but the exact geographic location of the boundry line was not conclusively and completely worked out until this century -1925. The wording of the treaty was the cause of the confusion, and the responsibility lay with such historic greats as Benjamin Franklin, John Adams, and John Jay. In 1842, Daniel Webster, representing the United States, and Lord Ashburton, representing British interests, were still trying to straighten it out.

Franklin, Adams, and Jay were among those negotiating in behalf of the United States at the time the Treaty of Paris was written. After a number of proposals and counter-proposals, the British ministry suggested that the boundry line from Lake Superior west follow "the usual water communication to Lake of the Woods, thence through the said lake to the most northwestern part thereof, and from thence on a due west course to the river Mississippi. . ." All this would have been fine except for one "minor detail" - the Mississippi River does not lie west of the Lake of the Woods; in fact, the source of the great river is about 140 miles south of the lake! The negotiators of the treaty had made the mistake of relying on "Mitchell's Map of North America," published in London in 1775. This map showed the Lake of the Woods as an oblong body of water with a regular shoreline and containing nine islands. Furthermore, it showed the Mississippi River as west of the lake.[1] It also showed the Lake draining east to Lake Superior instead of north to Hudson Bay.

Shortly after the signing of the treaty, the British became aware of the problem. As the Treaty of Ghent was being negotiated, they proposed that boundary negotiations be reopened and that the line be redefined from Lake Superior to the Mississippi. The government of the United States acknowledged the problem but said that it was not interested in dropping the border south of Lake of the Woods to the river. Agreement was finally reached, however, on the need to locate the most northwest point on the Lake of the Woods and its relationship to the Mississippi. It is interesting to speculate how a great deal of the history of Canada and the United States (and even the world) might have been changed if the British position had prevailed and the line had been drawn from Lake Superior to the Mississippi, thus giving almost the entire iron range of Minnesota to Canada! The industrial growth and power of the United States would

[1]Actually, an insert on the map covered part of the area and it was assumed the Mississippi River originated in Canada.

have been seriously stunted without these vast resources.

The treaty following the War of 1812 also specified that the boundary between Canada and the United States west of the Lake of the Woods should follow the 49th parallel.

An International Commission was finally appointed to resolve the border problems. In 1817 scientists, surveyors, astronomers, and others representing both governments began their study in the east - in Nova Scotia and Maine. They worked their way west to our *Canoe County* by 1823. Although they functioned as separate teams there was considerable communication. When they began their deliberations in the Minnesota-Ontario region, the British representation included David Thompson and Dr. John Bigsby, and the American contingent included Major Joseph Delafield, William Ferguson, and George Washington Whistler - the father of the famous artist. In the same year (1823), the United States government sent a party under the command of Major Stephen Long to determine and mark out the exact location of the 49th parallel, west of Lake of the Woods.

Delafield published his diaries under the title, "The Unfortified Boundary." Bigsby also published his account of the commission's work; it was entitled "Shoe and Canoe."

Long's work was relatively easy compared to the problems faced by the others. About all the two teams could agree on was Rainy River as a common boundary. They were unable to cope with the irregular shoreline and all the peninsulas, bays and islands of the Lake of the Woods in trying to determine the "most northwest point" on the lake. They were also unable to agree on the "usual water communication" from Lake Superior to Rainy River. The British maintained that it was the Pigeon River route, starting with Grand Portage. Major Delafield, speaking for the United States, insisted it was the Kaministikwia River route, beginning at Fort William on Thunder Bay. In retrospect, a better case can probably be made for the American position in that the French had long used the Kaministikwia route (particularly after the days of LaVèrendye) and the British also used this route after abandoning Grand Partage about 1802. Nevertheless, the boundary remained in dispute until 1842 when Daniel Webster and Lord Ashburton agreed on the Pigeon River route as the "usual water communication" from Lake Superior, west. They also agreed that the historic voyageur portages should be used in common by both countries - and they are to this day.

In 1841, the British appointed Dr. I. L. Tiarks, an astronomer, to try to locate the most northwest point on the Lake of the Woods. After considerable study, he finally took a map of the lake and a ruler. He placed the ruler across the lake at an exact NE to SW direction and then slowly moved it to the left across the map. He determined that the last point of shoreline touched by the ruler as it moved away from the lake would be the northwest point. Once the northwesern most point was established by Dr. Tiarks, he dropped a line straight south to the 49th parallel, thus creating the Northwest Angle of the United States. His decision was accepted by both sides, but it wasn't until 1872 that this point was finally announced as 29 23', 50.28 latitude and 95 08', 56.7 longitude. The sometimes irregular boundary line between the Mouth of the Rainy River and the northwest point was worked out separately, thus deciding which islands would be American and which Canadian. But it wasn't until 1925 that both countries agreed on all points - thus, finally completing the longest, continuous, unguarded boundary in the world.

CHAPTER FIVE
The Wolseley Expedition

The year 1870 was of considerable significance in the history of our **Canoe Country** and the Canadian West. The previous year (1869) Louis Riel had given leadership to an uprising of settlers in the Red River area. Although branded an outlaw and eventually hanged, he is considered quite a hero today. These people were concerned about the transfer of land (on which they were living) from the Hudson's Bay Company to the Canadian Government. They lost their homesteads without any means of appeal. The threat of settlers taking the law into their own hands aroused sufficient concern on the part of the Dominion Government to send Lt. Col. John Garnet Wolseley with a contingent of 1200 men to that area via our canoe country. The small army included 350 regulars from the 60th rifles or Royal Americans; the balance were "irregulars" including guides and boatsmen.

With so large a force, restoring order on the frontier would be no problem,[1] but moving more than a thousand men with all their equipment across the Canadian wilderness was no small challenge. Because this was a military expedition they could not travel the usual and easier route along the Minnesota border, nor could they use the route most freight was taking in that day, namely via the Twin Cities up the Minnesota River to the Red River and then north to what is now the Winnipeg area. Although they traveled an established route, (from Fort William up the Kaministikwia River, joining the old Grand Portage route via Lac La Croix and Rainy Lake) the size of the army made it necessary to literally carve a path through the Canadian wilderness. After a grueling three-month journey, they arrived at Rat Portage (Kenora) August 14, 1870. They had come all the way from Toronto in huge boats, each large enough to carry twenty men and all their personal equipment and provisions. The boats were portaged near Keewatin to the Winnipeg River. The remainder of the journey to Lake Winnipeg was comparitively easy.

The real significance of the expedition lay in the fact that law and order had come to the West. Colonel Wolseley had demonstrated that a sizeable military force could be moved across the wilderness whenever necessary and lawlessness would not be tolerated. However, the travel difficulties of the expedition were a dramatic demonstration of the need for improvement of the first Dawson route. Soon, hereafter, portages were improved, roads were built, and work was begun on a canal and locks which would have made portaging around Koochiching Falls on the Rainy River unnecessary -

[1]Faced with overwhelming odds, Riel and his followers fled - to fight another day and eventually lose.

if they had been completed.

Work on the proposed canal and locks brought a sizeable crew of men to what is now the International Falls-Fort Frances area and after the projects were abandoned, many stayed on as settlers. In all, the Canadian Government spent a million and a quarter dollars developing the original Dawson Trail.

Col. Wolseley's Red River Expedition by Francis Ann Hopkins   Credit: Public Archives of Canada

CHAPTER SIX
INDIAN TREATIES
AND LAND CESSIONS

Both the Canadian and the United States governments felt the need to work out a legal basis for land ownership with the Indians who had been on this continent for thousands of years before the coming of the first white man. Even though there was no question the white man had taken over, it was deemed necessary that some legal agreement, binding on both parties, be worked out between the government and the Indians. The government wanted a clear and legal title to the lands. In return, they would pay the Indians sums of money and offer guarantees of peace, protection, education, etc. It was important to the conscience and image of both the United States and Canadian governments that the Indians enter into such an agreement of their own free will. At the very least, it had to appear that way. Purchase agreements validated by treaties were the usual method used.

In the Canadian portion of our *Canoe Country*, the coming of Colonel Wolseley and his army of 1200 men in 1870 left little doubt in the minds of either the Indians or the whites who was in control of the country. Prior to that time, all attempts to work out a written agreement with the Indians as to which areas would be reserved for them and which would belong to the Dominion government were futile. We know that the government had long since assumed ownership of this entire area and had even parceled out much of it to the Hudson's Bay Company in 1870. The show of strength by Wolseley no doubt had a significant effect on the Indians and helped bring them to terms.

The Indian must have realized that he really had little choice when faced with the overwhelming and industrially supported forces of the "invaders." About all he had going for him was the conscience of his adversary. We have seen how the Indians trusted the French. No doubt the treaties would have been more easily arranged if Canada had still been in the hands of France.

The Indian Treaty of 1873 (the third in Canada but the first in this area) was concerned with the general area from Lake Superior to Manitoba. It is believed that at that time there were about 14,000 Indians living in this region - which encompassed about 55,000 square miles.

Negotiating the treaty was no easy task. There were many independent tribes in the area and several chiefs - each of whom considered himself sovereign over his particular domain. It was very difficult, therefore, to strike an agreement among the Indians. Year after year the meetings between the government and the chiefs were postponed - until

September, 1873. The conference finally took place on the North West Angle. Representing the government were: Alexander Morris, the Lieutenant Governor of Manitoba and the North West Territories; Lt. Colonel Provencher, representing the military; and S.J. Dawson, the explorer and now a member of parliament from Algoma. The official government delegation arrived on September 25th and took up headquaters at the Hudson's Bay Post; the Indians had already been in conference for several days.[1] We find this interesting description in the diary of a soldier, probably one of Provencher's men:

> *"Arrived Sept. 25. The governor of Manitoba arrived at 3:30. They mustered in Great force with squaws, papooses, etc. They marched around our camp headed by an old fellow in a soldier's coat and a Plug hat who looked like a broken-down admiral of the "Blue" with the jimjams. Their music consisted of four drums. They sang songs. . .The master of ceremonies wore a glaring red shirt with no sleeves, a plug hat, and white calico trousers. The clothing of most of the other braves was fancy but slight, consisting chiefly of nothing."*
> *"September 26. The Indians do not seem anxious to get to business. However, I do not blame them, for as long as they can make the affair last, the government is bound to supply them with food, etc. The way the gourmandized is simply alarming. Already two deaths from this cause has been reported.*
> *"October 1. The assembled braves during the pow wow would grunt incessantly, this to denote approbation, and when anything was mentioned about edibles, the grunting was terrible."*

We often think of the historic Indian as a quiet man of few words. Actually he was often eloquent and quite poetic and when his words have been recorded by historians they have demonstrated both wisdom and beauty. Lest we leave the impression from the foregoing quotation that the Indians communicated only by grunts and gestures, let us look at some quotations taken from the archives of the Department of Indian Affairs at Ottawa. We who love the **Canoe Country** can understand the Indians' love for this area, but imagine the trauma they felt as they realized they were giving up all legal claim to their home and the home of their ancestors. Apart from certain reservations, they were about to become guests in their own land. Listen!

> *Lt. Governor Morris: "Wood and water were the gifts of the Great Spirit, and were made alike for the White and the Red Man."*
> *Pow-wa-sang: "What you say of the rivers and trees is quite true, but it was the Indians' country and not the White Man's."*
> *Ma-we-d-pe-nais: "The Great Spirit has planted us on this ground where we are - as you were where you came from. We think where we are is our property. He gave us rules to govern ourselves properly."*
> *Kee-ta-kay-pi-nais: "The sound of the rustling of gold is under my feet where I stand. we have a rich country. It is the Great Spirit who gave us this - where we stand upon is Indian property and belongs to them."*
> *Chief Sah-Katch-eway: "We are the first that were planted here; we would ask you to assist us with every kind of implement to use for our benefit, to enable us to perform our work, a little of everything and money. We would borrow your cattle, I will find thereon to feed them. The waters out of which you sometimes take food for yourselves we will lend you in return. If you give what I ask, the time may come when*

[1]Reports indicate that more than 1000 Indians may have been on hand.

I will ask you to lend me one of your daughters and one of your sons to live with us, and in return I will lend you one of my daughters and one of my sons for you to teach what is good, and after they have learned, to teach us."

Chief Pa-pa-ska-gin: "Listen to what I am going to say to you my brothers. We ask you not to reject some of our children who have gone out of our place; they are scattered all over. A good tasted meat has drawn them away and we wish to draw them all here to be contented with us. I would not like that anyone of my children should not eat meat with me."

Chief Go-bay: "We ask that the Indians may not have to pay their passage on the fire boats and the things that run swiftly by fire, but can go free and we must have the privilege to travel about the country where it is empty. we do not want anyone to mark out our reserves; we have already marked them out."

Chief Canda-com-iga-wi-innie: "You understand me now. I have taken your hand firmly and in friendship. I repeat twice that I have done so and with these promises you have made let the treaty be made. Let it be as you have promised for as long as the sun rises over our heads and as long as the water runs. One thing that deranges my kettle a litte; in this land where food for our substance used to be plentiful, I perceive it has gone scarce. We wish that the river be left as it was found from the beginning - that nothing be broken."

On October 3, 1873, when the treaty was finally consumated and about to be signed, Chiefs Ma-we-d-pe-nais and Oaw-wa-sand spoke to Governor Morris thus as representatives of their people:

"Now we stand before you all. What has been done here today has been done openly before the Great Spirit and before the Nation. Never let anyone say it has been done secretly and in closing this Council I take off my glove and in giving you my hand I hold fast all the promises you have made and I hope they will last as long as the sun goes round and the water flows as you have said."

Governor Morris said in reply:

"I accept your hand and with it the lands and will keep all my promises, in the firm belief that the treaty now to be signed will bring the Red Man and the White Man together as friends forever."

The Treaty in its entirety as well as the orders establishing the negotiating commission is reproduced in the appendix of the book, "Lake of the Woods, Yesterday and Today," by this author. The concessions, cash settlements, and goods promised the Indians - as well as the pledges extracted in return - make especially interesting reading. For example, each chief was promised "an appropriate suit of clothes" every three years. Many Canadians living in the border country can recall the blue serge suits which came to identify the chiefs. Although the treaty is not followed "to the letter," cash settlements are still made twice each year.

Meanwhile, the United States Government was in the process of negotiating treaties with the Ojibway and Sioux of Minnesota. There were ten separate agreements reached between 1830 and 1889 and the dozens of boundry lines made a map of Minnesota look very much like a patch-work quilt. In the boundry waters area there were three separte agreements, all with the Ojibway:

(1) 1854 - the entire Arrowhead Region including Duluth,
(2) 1866 - a much smaller area south of Rainy and other border lakes:
(3) 1889 - the area south of Lake of the Woods and Rainy River.

The following is an exerpt from the 1866 Treaty between the U.S. Government and the Nett Lake Bands, creating the Nett Lake Reservation:

> *The United States agrees to erect, on the Nett Lake reserve, the following named buildings: one blacksmith shop, to cost not exceeding five hundred dollars; one schoolhouse, to cost not exceeding five hundred dollars; and eight horses for their chiefs, to cost not exceeding four hundred dollars each; and a building for an agency house and store-house to cost not exceeding two thousand dollars.*
>
> *Also for the support of the blacksmith and his outfit, fifteen hundred dollars annually, for twenty years; for school purposes eight hundred dollars; for farming tools and instruction in farming, eight hundred dollars; for annuity payment, eleven thousand dollars, partly in cash and partly in goods.*
>
> *Also thirty thousand dollars for presents to the chiefs and to the people upon the ratification of this treaty; and not to exceed ten thousand dollars for the expenses of transportation and subsistence of the Indian delegates who visited Washington for the purpose of negotiating this treaty.*

The Nett Lake Ojibway were somewhat isolated from the other bands and at times seemed to have been bypassed by the fur trade activity. The village site at the mouth of the Vermilion River was first occupied by the Ojibway in 1736 by a group migrating from the big LaPoint settlement. Nothing is further recorded of their history, however, until the Trading season of 1804-05 when Hugh Faries of the Northwest Company reported his activities as well as those of competitive traders operating in this area. Nett Lake may have been the first permanent Ojibway settlement in Minnesota and probably served as the source of other settlements along the border area.

With the 1889 purchase, only the Red Lake area remained in Indian hands in Minnesota. Much pressure was applied on the Red Lake band by both the Land Commission[1] and other Indians who flaunted their new found (though short lived) wealth - but the leadership held firm, and retained an area about the size of Rhode Island, which remains legally independent of the United States to this day. The details of these negotiations are recalled in the book, "Tales of Four Lakes and a River,"[2] by this author.

Much has been written by white man about the acquisition of Indian territories, but here is an Indian point of view of how our continents' first residents must have felt about the coming of the whites - as expressed by Lolita Taylor, a Wisconsin Ojibway, in her book, ***The Native American:***[3]

> *"Before the signing of the Treaty of 1837 the Ojibwa were told and distinctly understood they would retain possession of their land - that the Government wanted only the mineral rights and the pine. The people were to remain on the land as long as they behaved themselves and caused no trouble. They never knew that they had ceded away their land until told to move in 1849. Now they were to leave their homes and the graves of their loved ones and go to a reservation. "Who has been misbehaving?" they asked and even traveled around to see if they could find anyone who had been causing trouble.*
>
> *Older Indians were beginning to see what was happening at last. "They are as*

[1]U.S. Commission members at that time were Henry Rice of Minnesota, Bishop Martin Marty of North Dakota, and Joseph Whiting of Wisconsin. Consultants were Bishop Whipple and Archbishop Ireland.

[2]The four lakes included in the history are Leech Lake, Mille Lacs Lake, Gull Lake, and the Red Lakes; the River is the Crow Wing.

[3]Taylor, Lolita, ***The Native American, 1976.***

TREATIES BETWEEN MINNESOTA INDIAN TRIBES
AND THE UNITED STATES GOVERNMENT[1]

CEDED IN
1863
(OLD
CROSSING
TREATY)

CEDED IN 1889

CEDED IN
1866

CHIPPEWA CEDED
IN 1854

CHIPPEWA CEDED
IN 1855
TREATY

CHIPPEWA
CEDED IN
1847

SIOUX, CHIPPEWA
GAVE UP TRIANGLE
IN 1837 TREATY

SIOUX KEPT
SMALL TRACTS IN
1851 TREATY

SET ASIDE FOR SIOUX
HALF-BREEDS, BUT
UNOCCUPIED; U.S.
PURCHASED IT LATER

CEDED IN 1851 IN TREATIES OF
TRAVERSE DES SIOUX & MENDOTA

CEDED IN 1830 IN TREATY SIGNED AT
PRAIRIE DU CHIEN

[1]Red Lake Reserve not shown.

thick as the trees in the forest" they said. "They are killing our game, they are destroying the home of the deer and the bear." They shook their heads in despair as they saw the logs tearing the rice beds out of the rivers. "It won't be long before rice goes the way of the pine trees," they said. It was truly spoken. Farmers anxious to get their plows into the ground often burned off large tracts of ground to clear it for fields. Hills that should never have been cut over were left bare to erode in the wind and rain. Cattle grazed on the river banks and along the sparkling trout streams sending dirt and filth into the waters and taking away the natural cover to let rains wash silt down the banks.

To an outsider this may have seemed a bit extreme, but to the Ojibwa it was a real blow. Yet he must bow to the intruder. In many cases it was the policy of the land owner (now the white man) to complain of his Indian neighbor simply to have him removed. Land grabbers came into the country and misrepresented their rights by saying they had title to swamp lands or to land set aside for schools. In this way they gained control of much of the cranberry beds. Where railroad companies paid for the right of way through the white man's land, they simply diregarded the Indian's. Records say "they are squatters." Yes they were squatters on their own land.

Gradually the Ojibwa's life bagan to change. He no longer could be a logger - there were no more logs to float down the streams. His sources of food were yielding less and less. No longer could he depend on his furs, since he was subject to the white man's conservation laws that prohibited him from trapping except at certain times. Where he had once felt rich and secure in the gifts of the Great Spirit he now became insecure. And he began to distrust not only the culture that had done this to him, but his own way of life.

The Priest gave him to understand that he was living a life of sin. What had become of all the gentle ones he had known before? Were they damned because the Priest had been too late to save them? What had happened to the proud ancestors and their island sanctuary?

The educator told him he was ignorant. Not only that, his parents were ignorant, too. They were talking the wrong language, they were wearing the wrong kinds of clothes. Never mind that the European came to this country bathless - the Indian was the one called dirty.

The farmer and the industrialist called him lazy. They just couldn't understand why the Indian wasn't out to get all the money for himself. They had no idea of sharing as the Ojibwa did.

His land had been taken because it was valuable to the European. So were his forests, his furs, wild rice and game. How much more could a being endure?"

It is little wonder that the Canadian and American Treaties, signed back in the 1800's, are still very much in the news today.

CHAPTER SEVEN
Gold!

Down through the centuries the cry of "gold" has excited man beyond all reason. The prospect of quick riches has divided families, taken men across continents, separated them from their jobs, and usually ended more in poverty than in wealth. But we have never learned.

And so it was when gold was discovered in our boundry waters canoe area that thousands rushed into the wilderness with a dream of quickly making their fortune. In the case of the gold rushes on Rainy Lake and on Lake of the Woods at the close of the last century, only a handful of prospectors ended up with anything to show for their efforts. A few corporate endeavors were more successful, but most of these were north and east of Lake of the Woods. Actually, we can be thankful the mining operations were not more productive, or our beloved wilderness area would long ago have given away to industrial development.

But while it lasted, the gold rush was as genuine as any on this continent, and may have lasted longer had not the promise of greater wealth developed in Alaska and along the Yukon. Also, the hard-rock mining of our *Canoe Country* called for a great deal more hard labor than the pan and sluice box which were so successful in the Northwest.

We are not quite sure when or how it all began, but the first strike may have been on Lake Vermilion in 1865, when hundreds rushed north - mostly by way of Minnesota -and tried their luck all around the lake. Activity mushroomed but died almost as quickly when the operation proved relatively unproductive.

Meanwhile, a surveyor for the Canadian Pacific Railroad, Captain Walpole Roland, found traces of gold near Rat Portage (Kenora), and when the rails were laid from Eastern Canada to Lake of the Woods (and on to Winnipeg) in the early 1880's, a gold rush was inevitable. Mining operations developed in all directions from Rat Portage - including the lake itself. By 1894, E. Arnold, the proprietor of Russell House in that city, boasted of thirty mines in operation within twenty-two miles of the hotel. The Mikado and Gold Coin mines were established on Shoal Lake (the northwest portion of Lake of the Woods), the Sultana and Master Jack were in operation on the north end of the Lake near Rat Portage, and the Regina and La Massicote were in production on Whitefish Bay. Meanwhile, individual prospectors swarmed all over the Lake of the Woods. However, by 1900, most operations had moved away from the lake itself to

Little America Gold Mine, Rainy Lake   Courtesy Minnesota Historical Society

the north and east of Rat Portage. The declining value of gold closed most of the mines in this century, but recent increases in value and new discoveries around Red Lake (Ontario), Pickel Crow, Trout Lake, and Stanley Lake have once again made Kenora a center for mining activities.

Discoveries of gold were made in the Rainy Lake region as early as 1875 when George Stuntz prospected the shores of Loon Lake (just east of Rainy Lake). But it was George Davis who caused the most excitement after spending a July night in 1893 alone on Little America Island on Rainy Lake and, the next morning, successfully panned some flakes of gold out of a vein of quartz. As always, the news of the dicovery of gold spread like wildfire, and when the ice went out on Rainy Lake the next spring, the village of Rainy Lake City was born (about twelve miles east of the present site of International Falls). By late summer the mining camp had become a wilderness metropolis of more than 500 citizens. It even boasted its own newspaper: the "Rainy Lake Journal," which told of a business community which included "three general stores, a hardware store, 3 hotels, a barber shop, two restaurants, a post office, and 5 saloons." The meat counters specialized in wild game (there was little choice) with the entire carcass of a moose selling for $5.00, a caribou for $2.00 and a deer for $1.00 - while walleyes, whitefish, and northerns went for a nickel each.[1]

Mining operations quickly sprang up all over the lake and on the Seine River. In addition to "Big American" on Dryweed Island, there were such unlikely names as "Lucky Coon," "Mastadon," "Joe La Course," "Red Gut," "Lucella," "Alice A.," "Madelaine," "Little Canada," "Bad Vermilion," "Wiggins," "Gold Harbor," "Holman," "Lyle," and "Bushy Head."

[1]Grace Lee Nute, *Rainy River Country*, M. H. S.,

A significant news item in an 1894 edition of the "Rainy Lake Journal" told of the founding of the village of Koochiching on the site of present day International Falls.

Logging operations were begun in the Lake of the Woods-Rainy River-Rainy Lake region concurrently with the gold rush, and a saw mill at Rainy Lake city prolonged the community's life for a time, but as the prospectors left or converted into lumberjacks, the wilderness city was doomed to die. By 1906 only a single, die-hard citizen remained.

The mines themselves were returned to the wilderness. Almost sacrilegiously, the tailings of the Little America mine were used to firm-up the mirey streets of a new boom town, International Falls.

Although the first prospectors came by canoe, the gold rush helped to build steamboat traffic in the border region. Though the gold mines perished, the steamboats stayed on to serve the loggers and the Rainy River farmers. The "Libby" became a fixture on Lake Vermilion and the "May Carter" on Crane Lake. By 1890, scores of steamboats sent up their clouds of black smoke as they cruised between ports on Lake of the Woods and Rainy Lake. They had such picturesque names as "Lady of the Lake,"[1] "The Shamrock," "Edna Bridges," "Daisy Moore," "The Keenora," "Agwinde," "Monarch," "Empress," "D. L. Mather," "City of Alberton," "Verbena," "Sir William Van Horne," and "Na Ma Puk." It has been estimated that in 1890, no less than twenty-one steamers sailed regularly between Rat Portage (Kenora) and Fort Frances.

The rates were relatively high, considering the value of the dollar in that day. Frank Yeigh, in his publication entitled **The Rainy River District,** quoted the fare on the "Shamrock" from Rat Portage to Fort Frances at $4.00 for adults and $2.50 for children. Cattle and horses were also $4.00 a head; household goods went for $8.00 per ton; and general supplies at $8.00 a ton.

The most significant by-product of the gold rush was the discovery of iron in northern Minnesota. George Stuntz, for example, who was among the first prospectors for gold, found iron ore on his way north. When mining began in earnest on the Mesabi and Vermilion ranges, the recollections of the earlier gold miners hastened the opening of the country. The operations at Tower and Ely were at the very doorstep of our wilderness canoe area. The great open pit iron mines of the Mesabi range were developed less than 100 miles to the south. The first underground mine was at Soudan; it is now a unique and most interesting state park.

Iron and gold are not the only metallic resource found in the area. Even while the gold rush was in progress, the Royal Commission on the Mineral Resources of Ontario reported deposits of commercial value of silver, copper and zinc along the Canadian side of the border. In addition, there are large reserves of nickel and copper on the American side of the border.

The years of 1856 and '57 saw a rush of copper prospectors up the north shore of Lake Superior. Because of the Panic of 1857 and because the prospecting had not been particularly fruitful, most ceased their operations within the year. During the Civil War there was a renewed interest in copper in the same area but these efforts also pro-

[1]The "Lady of the Lake" was the first steamboat to sail out of Rat Portage. It was 115 ft. long and began its service as a side-wheeler. Later it was converted to a sternwheel operation. It was dismantled in 1880.

[2]Yeigh, Frank, **The Rainy River District,** Warinch and Sors, Toronto, 1860.

ved to be unproductive.

It is interesting that the Public Works report for the Dominion (Canada) in 1875 stated, "The Indians, both of Rainy Lake and the Lake of the Woods have among them specimens of native gold and silver ore, which they affirm to be found in places known to them in abundance." We know, too, that copper artifacts - dating back to 2000 B.C., have been found in Indian burial mounds along Rainy Lake. So really, who were the first miners in our *Canoe Country?*

There is little doubt that metallic resources of considerable commercial value lie within our remaining wilderness canoe area. Hopefully, we will always recognize the even greater value of the recreational resources which are found above ground.

CHAPTER EIGHT
Then Came the Lumberjacks

The lumberjacks of the north country have given us a heritage nearly as romantic and legendary as that of the voyageurs. The stories of Paul Bunyan are, of course, delightful in their exaggeration; nevertheless, the logger was in his own way a genuine hero of the north woods. He provided the lumber with which we built two nations. A rapidly growing United States and Canada needed schools and homes and churches and shops and industrial buildings; the forests of North America seemed to contain an endless source of oak, pine, birch, maple, cedar, and spruce with which to do the job.

It is tempting for us, in retrospect, to think of the lumberjack as a villain who denuded the landscape and exposed the earth to erosion. But before we treat him too harshly we must realize -

* The lumber was essential to the building of two new countries,
* That the people of that day viewed the supply as endless,
* That is was common to work a ten hour day and a six day week with no vacations - only an occasional holiday - and little thought was given, therefore, to the recreational value of the forests,
* That land had to be cleared to plant crops to feed a new, industrialized society, and
* That it was assumed the forests would grow back - and they did (although in many areas we traded the noble pines for scrub oak and popple).

True, management could have planned better; it was not necessary to rape the beautiful shorelines of lakes and rivers; and more thought should have been given to the future. But all that is now history - and because of the circumstances of that time, which we have just cited, we must not judge the logger of another generation by the standards of today. The lumberjack was only doing his job and doing it well.

The logging camp was a unique community out of our nation's past, a chapter in our history well worth remembering. The lumberjack worked in a remarkable setting, particularly those who labored in our canoe country. Besides the beauty of the rivers, lakes, and islands, there was an abundance of wildlife. In addition to the animals and birds found in the region today, the last of the elk[1] and caribou were still to be seen. In

[1]A small herd of elk is still to be found near Baudette.

the early years of logging history along the boundry waters (the late 1800's) the Indian still lived much as he had for generation and the lumberjack was privileged to see his lodges and birchbark canoes. And the last of the voyageurs could also be seen - and heard.

All logging camps were not alike - but just about. For a contingent of from one hundred to a hundred and fifty men there were usually three bunkhouses, a cooking shack, an office and supply headquarters, a shelter for the horses, a blacksmith shop and forge, a shanty where saws were sharpened, and a root cellar for storing vegetables. Construction was usually of rough pine (mainly Norway) and meant to be temporary. When an area was logged out, only the windows, doors, frames, and hardware were salvaged and moved to the new location. Two or three years was the average life of a logging camp.

The bunkhouses were long and narrow with double-deck beds lining both walls. Tradition has it that Pullman designed his railroad sleeping cars after visiting a logging camp bunkhouse. Winters were often bitter cold and the only source of heat was a pot-bellied or barrel stove stationed in the aisle between the bunks. Insulation was not used and it was not unusual for a logger to awaken in the morning with his hair frozen to the frost-covered wall! Lines were strung near the ceiling for drying clothing, perhaps more wet with sweat than moisture from the snow. No doubt the aroma added to the atmosphere! And yet, it is said the teamsters were housed separately near the horse barn because they smelled like their animals. On very cold days, the lumberjacks were inclined to wear more than one suit of long underwear and it was customary on those occasions to wear the clean suit next to the skin and pull on the used suit over the other. Lice were a problem in many logging camps and were sometimes so bad the men gave up fighting them and just learned to live with them.

The lumberjacks were of mixed heritage. The early logger on the Minnesota side came from as far east as New England and fresh out of the Michigan and Wisconsin woods. Likewise, the first Canadian loggers came from the east. But on both sides of the border, "locals" soon joined the crews and made for a real "melting pot" of all nationalities. Most were first generation North Americans providing an interesting mixture of brogues and accents.

By testimony of old lumberjacks, life in the logging camps was nowhere near as boisterous as portrayed in movies or legend. Spending all of the daylight hours at hard work, six days a week, left little energy for rowdyism. Furthermore, alcohol was strictly forbidden in most camps. In fact, alcoholics were known to "take the cure" by going to work in the woods. Although many smoked, "chewing" was more common: the men needed both hands free in their work. Card playing was a favorite evening pastime; dry beans often substituted for poker chips. Sundays meant "wash day" (usually outside) and relaxation.

In this harsh environment, mealtime was really something to look forward to. In contrast with the voyageurs who survived on minimal rations, the lumberjacks enjoyed excellent food and plenty of it. Meat was served at every meal and included ham, fresh beef and veal, bologna, wieners, salt pork, pork sausage, bacon, and liver. Fish and wild game added still more variety.

Bunkhouse, J. M. Paine Logging Camp, 1899   Courtesy Minnesota Historical Society

Logging Camp Dining Hall - Pine Island Area (1900-1902)   Courtesy Minnesota Historical Society

Vegetables were limited to those which could be stored such as potatoes, cabbage, carrots, rutabagas, onions, and parsnips. Beans were prepared in iron kettles or baked in the oven.

Breads, cakes, doughnuts, and pies were baked fresh daily.

While breakfast and supper were served in the camp, the noon meal was often brought out to the men by sleigh or "swingdingle." Although the food was usually more than adequate, the table setting was austere - with tin plates and cups and metal utensils (steel, but not stainless). Traditionally, meals were eaten in silence - to save time and to preserve the peace.

A welcome break in camp routine was the occasional visit of a circuit rider preacher or "sky pilot." Some became legends in their own right. Among those who were better known to the loggers of *Canoe Country* were Frank Higgins, John Sorenberger (a former boxer lead to the Lord by Higgins), and "Jerusalem Slim." Higgins, the best known and perhaps most effective of the three, received his spiritual training at Hamline University in St. Paul (Methodist) but served first in a Presbyterian church - in Annandale, Minnesota. Nearly all of his preaching career was spent in the northwoods, walking from camp to camp with a heavy packsack on his back - which eventually lead to his death - cancer of the collarbone. Preacher Higgins was short, but heavy and muscular, and he was not beyond manhandling an irreverent lumberjack now and then. He was well known for his strong singing voice and the men reportedly looked forward to joining in the familiar hymns.

Most loggers were family men who looked at their job as just another way of making a living and supported a wife and kids in some town farther south - where they would return come spring. Although some men stayed on for the drives down rivers and across lakes, logging was mostly a winter occupation. Swamps and hoards of flies and mosquitoes were too much to cope with in summer. Besides, it was much easier to skid the heavy logs over snow than across bare ground. After spring break-up, the teamsters took their horses and headed south to work on roads and farms. Actually, most horses came out of the Red River Valley and were leased.

Lest we leave the impression lumberjacks were without sin, let us hasten to add that most made up for their regulated camp life when they hit town on holidays or at the end of the logging season. Frontier towns were crowded with saloons and brothel houses and many a man blew his stake in a matter of hours. Most northern Minnesota towns owe their origin to saw mills and nearby logging operations - and they were all pretty wild! Boom towns which served our border area included Fort Frances, Koochiching (or International Fall as it was called after 1904), Ranier, Baudette, Spooner (now part of Baudette), Beaver (now Rainy River), Tower, Ely, Virginia, Deer River and Grand Marais.

In our *Canoe Country,* Lake of the Woods was the first to be logged; Rainy River and Rainy Lake came next. This is because the first railroad in the area came to Rat Portage and Keewatin Mills on its way from Montreal to Winnipeg. John Mather, one of the financial pioneers of the early Canadian West, was associated with the coming of both the railroad and the lumbering industry to the Lake of the Woods.

When the Bank of Ottawa was established in 1874, Mather was elected to its Board of Directors. As his interests moved west he was instrumental in establishing a branch

Lunch in the woods, served by a "Swingdingle"   Courtesy Minnesota Historical Society

Spring comes to Dermutt's Logging Camp - 1890   Courtesy Minnesota Historical Society

bank in Winnipeg and later in the two frontier villages which developed out of the Rat Portage trading posts.

Mather had a contract with the Canadian Pacific Railroad to provide timbers for the ties and trestles. He began operating the first sawmill on the Lake of the Woods in 1880. His first contract was with Peter Campbell who was to "cut all the pine, spruce, and tamarack" on Tunnel Island, Rat Portage. Opening the mill was no easy task. Just getting the equipment from Minneapolis to the site of present day Kenora was a monumental ordeal. The heavy machinery had to be carried up the Minnesota River, down the Red River to Winnipeg, and across country by wagon and sleds to the North West Angle (over the Dawson Trail). Barges were then constructed for the final leg of the journey to the north end of the lake.

Other mills soon sprang up in the Rat Portage and Keewatin Mills area and during the next decade logging operations spread over most of the Lake of the Woods. Timber was harvested from points as far away as the tributaries of the Rainy River (including the Vermilion, Rat Root, Little Fork, Big Fork, and Rapid Rivers on the Minnesota side and the Pune, Sturgeon, and Vallee Rivers on the Canadian side). All of these logs were transported to the mills at the north end of the lake.

Actually, the taking of timber from the Minnesota side was illegal. It is estimated that some eighty-five million feet of lumber were poached annually from the United States from 1890-1900! The U.S. Government was aware of these operations as early as 1878. Agents were sent out each year to warn the violators, but cutting resumed as soon as the authorities left the area. By 1900 most of the big timber had been harvested. The Morris Act of 1902 made available much of the former Indian territories to white settlers. The diminished timber supply plus the fact that the United States Government took better care of the area when it was no longer "just Indian territory" brought an end to the timber poaching.

Loggers made good settlers, and with the coming of the railroad, the population of the Rat Portage - Keewatin Mills area grew rapidly. Prior to the coming of Col. Wolseley and his army in 1870, the north end of the lake had only a few trading posts and a handful of white men. With the coming of "law and order" a few more hardy souls and adventurers were drawn to the area. Even some of the Colonel's men fell in love with the lake and stayed on or returned when the expedition to Winnipeg was over. By 1881, with the coming of the railroad and the start of the lumbering industry, the Rat Portage area had an official population of 4,564!

All of this time, the southern part of the lake and the Minnesota side remained undeveloped, with the exception of the village of Northwest Angle. There was extensive cutting along the southern part of the lake, but all logs were floated to the north end to be milled. The nearest railroad to the south was still more than 80 miles away, terminating in Tower.

In 1900, rail service was finally extended to the south side of Lake of the Woods by means of the Canadian Northern Railway including Warroad, Baudette, and Fort Frances on its way from Winnipeg to Port Arthur (Thunder Bay).

Logging was big business and on the American side we find names like Weyerhaeuser, Backus, Pillsbury, Walker, Akeley, Brooks, and Cook. Individual empires gave way to corporate entities, some of which survive to this day. For example,

E.W. Backus was instrumental in the formation of a number of companies in the Rainy River area, including E.W. Backus and Co., The Koochiching Co., Backus and Brooks Co., The International Lumber Co., The International Improvement Co., the Keewatin Lumber Co., Ltd., The Columbia Gold Mining Co., The Rainy River Lumber Co., The National Pole and Treating Co., and the Minnesota and Ontario Paper Company (which survives as a part of Boise Cascade[1]).

Backus, through his Koochiching Company, was involved in the construction of the dam and bridge between International Falls and Fort Frances. After several years of planning and working out international legal problems, construction was begun in 1905. Within five years, the mighty falls which could once be heard as far as eight miles away had been incorporated into the dam and the water power had been harnessed by giant turbines.

The Minnesota and Ontario Paper Company (now part of Boise Cascade) had a near monopoly on logging operations in Koochiching County and from there west through one of its subsidiaries - the International Lumber Company. In its peak year (1917), twenty-three logging camps were in operation with a payroll of about 4000 men. Meanwhile, the area east of Koochiching County was under the control of a coalition of lumber magnates including Frederick Weyerhaeuser, Edward Hines, William O'Brien, and Wirt Cook. Their vehicle was the Virginia and Rainy Lake Lumber Company which was destined to become the largest of its kind in Minnesota. During the peak of the cutting season, about 2800 loggers were on the payroll with an additional 1700 employed in the huge Virginia mill (the world's largest white pine operation) and still others in the Duluth mill.

Huge hoists were in operation on several of the boundry waters lakes and rivers and were used to transfer the logs from the water to the railroad for shipment to Virginia, International Falls, and other mills; they included Rainy, Namakan, Kabetogama, Elbow, Black Duck, Johnson, Beaudoin, Ash, Elephant, and Echo.[1]

By 1907, railroad service from Minnesota finally reached International Falls - from two directions: The Minnesota and International from the south and the Duluth, Winnipeg and Pacific from the east. The "M & I" later became a part of the Northern Pacific (now Burlington Northern) and was encouraged to extend itself to International Falls by the Backus interests. The railroad from the east to Ranier and Fort Frances was actually an adjunct of the Virginia and Rainy Lake Lumber Company's logging road, extended with help from the Canadian Northern. Hundreds of miles of additional track were layed on both sides of the border to service the respective logging operations. A new village was founded 50 miles north of Virginia, called Cusson, as a hub for logging spur activities. Another hub created the village of Gheen between Cusson and Virginia (South of Orr).

In the 1900's steam powered vehicles other than the locomotive were developed to facilitate the actual logging operations; including power shovels, amphibious tugs (called "alligators"), and log haulers. Most of these unusual contraptions moved on caterpillar type tracks and are considered to be the predecessors of tanks and similar

[1]Grace Lee Nute, *Rainy River Country,* M. H. S.,

military vehicles.

After World War I, the logging industry became more highly mechanized. Horses began to give way to tractors and dozers and, eventually, to highly specialized and articulated equipment. Railroad spurs were ripped up and replaced with logging roads and trucks. By 1940, the transition to a fully mechanized industry was complete.

But by then the peak of activity had long since been reached and passed. The Virginia and Rainy Lake Lumber Company completed its operations in 1928 and the International Lumber Company was phased out by 1937. Logging has continued to the present - and has even increased in recent years as we experience the maturation of second growth forests. However, the corporate giants have been replaced by small companies and family and partnership operations. In much of our *Canoe Country*, the second growth forests and remaining stands of virgin timber are protected. In the Boundary Waters Canoe Area they are protected by federal legislation and in Voyageurs National Park by both federal and state laws. On the Canadian side, logging is regulated in the Quetico area and on Lake of the Woods. But through it all the lumberjack has earned his place as a legitimate hero of the northern wilderness.

CHAPTER NINE
The
Commercial Fisherman

Commercial fishing is still a legal and viable industry at both the east and west ends of our **Boundary Waters**: on Lake Superior and on Lake of the Woods. At one time, the entire length of the region included fishing for profit ventures to some degree. With the coming of tourism and legislation to preserve the wilderness, commercial fishing was outlawed first on Kabetogama, then Namakan, and later on Rainy Lake as well as the other bodies of water east to Lake Superior.

The Lake Superior fisheries suffered a severe setback with the coming of the sea lamprey in the late 1920's. This large and viscious parasite was particularly devastating to lake trout but had little effect on other species. Chemical controls administered at spawning time have been 90% effective, and, with the help of an ambitious restocking program, there is for the first time in many years promise for the sports fisherman and even for the return of more successful commercial ventures.

One of the first commercial fishing operations on Lake Superior was sponsored by the American Fur Company between 1835 and 1841 at Grand Portage and on Isle Royal. There was no problem in catching fish but marketing was another matter and the operations were abandoned for lack of a good outlet. Following the copper "rush" in 1856 and '57, settlements began to spring up all along the Lake Superior shoreline. Many of the settlers looked to commercial fishing for an income but had the same marketing problems as the American Fur Company. However, in 1870 two railroad companies began construction of lines from Duluth to St. Paul and to Brainerd (and later Staples where it joined the mainline to the west coast). The Lake Superior and Mississippi railroad and the Northern Pacific finally provided a market for the commercial fishermen.

Historically, the cisco (or chub)[1] was the major commercial fish from the late 1800's up to the 1920's. Meanwhile, herring production was on the increase and dominated the commercial take during the decades of the 20's and 30's. At one point, the Minnesota waters of Lake Superior produced about 78% of the total U.S. harvest. A serious decline in the herring population has taken place since the 1940's, but restrictions on netting during the spawning run and a restocking program bode well for the future.

Smelt first appeared in Lake Superior in 1946 and are currently the dominant commercial fishery. The taking of these little silvery fish commercially began in 1951 when

[1] There are 5 species of Ciscos or deep water chubs. Shallow water chubs are also called herring.

6000 pounds were harvested. The fishery has generally increased ever since with a record catch of 2.9 million pounds in 1976. Trawlers operate in the Duluth area but seining occurs all along the Minnesota shore as far north as Grand Portage. "Smelting" has become a spring tradition for many sports fishermen and they may be found with their dip nets at the mouths of most Lake Superior streams well into the night in late April and early May.

Netting Herring, Lake Superior, 1940   Courtesy Gallagher Studios, Duluth

Lake Trout, over the years, have been a prime target of commercial and sports fishermen alike. Minnesota waters yielded about 300,000 pounds of Lake Trout annually between 1920 and 1940. As we have already noted, the coming of the sea lamprey in the late 1940's was devastating to this great fish and the population was so depleted the season was closed in 1961. Control of the lamprey and restocking efforts since 1964 have been so successful, however, that commercial fishermen are now (1980) allowed to take (and tag) 7000 Lake Trout annually and sports fishermen are permitted a daily limit of three. Minnesota's Department of Natural Resources estimates the catch by sportsmen at slightly less than the commercial take. Some old timers on the lake insist there are more Lake Trout in Superior's waters now than at any time in their memory.

At this printing, about 40 licensed commercial fishermen operate in the Minnesota waters of Lake Superior. The number has varied over the years depending upon the supply and the market. It is interesting that there are more commercial fishermen on the lake today than there were in 1860 and 1870 when the census taken in those years reported 22 and 32 fishermen respectively.[1] Most of today's commercial fishermen are either Indians or descendants of the hardy Scandinavians who came here in the latter part of the 19th century, attracted by the rocky shores and timbered hills so much like their native Norway, Sweden and Finland. They settled the rugged Minnesota shoreline all the way from Duluth to Grand Portage including such communities as Two Harbors, Tofte, Lutsen, Grand Marais, and Hovland.

The Lake of the Woods has been the scene of continuous commercial fishing from the beginning and for its size has probably had more impact on the market than any lake on the continent. The practices we shall describe may be considered very similar to fishing operations once used on all boundary waters, although the species and proportions of species would vary some from lake to lake.

When LaVèrendye and his men built Fort St. Charles, they established a winter fishing camp (probably at the mouth of the Grassy River), so we know that they were partially dependent on the fish of the lake for survival. As, the Treaty of 1873 was negotiated between Her Majesties government and the Indians of the area, the chiefs expressed a concern that the fish supply was being depleted by the white man. Just as soon as the railroad made it possible to ship fish to eastern markets, netting fish for money began in earnest. Commercial fishing was identifiable as an industry on Lake of the Woods by 1885 when commercial pound nets were used for the first time. By 1896, more than 300 pound nets were in use in Minnesota and Ontario waters. The Minnesota Legislature first established commercial fishing regulations for Lake of the Woods in 1895. Commercial fishing has continued both in Canadian and United States waters to the present. At the turn of the century the usual price for northern pike was three cents a pound and four cents for walleyes. One early transaction involved seven sturgeon (the smallest of which was forty pounds) traded for one cotton shirt. In this century, there has been the ever increasing pressure of sports fishing and today - as if the fish didn't have trouble enough already with nets, guides, and irresistible lures of all descriptions - we now have electronic devices to indicate temperature, depth, and the very location of the fish themselves! Yet, through it all, fishing has remained excellent.

Although the total number of fish taken over the years has increased slightly the number of walleyes and northern pike taken by commercial fishing has diminished considerably in recent times. Much of the take is now rough fish.

Commercial fishing has had an effect on the fish population of the lake. We know from records kept on the Minnesota side of Lake of the Woods that there has been a dramatic change in the fish population over the years. Before the turn of the century, sturgeon made up over one-half of the commercial catch and Lake of the Woods was one of the continent's principal sources of this giant remnant of the glacial age. By 1920, they were all but extinct for commercial purposes. The whitefish population on Minnesota waters was so depleted by the late 1930's that it had no further commercial value. More restrictive legislation was adopted by the Minnesota legislature in 1941 setting size limits for sauger, walleye, northern pike, and whitefish. The taking of sturgeon, muskellunge, bass, and crappies by commercial means was outlawed altogether. Commercial fishermen were limited to the use of no more than six pound nets, 10 fyke nets,

[1]Kaups, Matti, North Shore Commercial Fishing, 1849-1870 "Minnesota History," summer 1978.

or 4,000 feet of gill nets. Both fishermen and fishermen's helpers were required to be licensed. The commercial fishing opening was set for June 1 of each year and certain parts of the lake were placed off limits so as to not conflict with sport fishing.

Most commercial fishing on Lake of the Woods is done as a family business with the "know how" passed along from generation to generation to generation.

Fishing gear is closely regulated. Gill nets, pound net, trap nets, and fyke nets are all legal, but each must meet specific criteria. For example, gill nets in Minnesota waters must have a minimum size of four inches stretched mesh and must not exceed a depth of 30 meshes. Incidentally, gill nets are the most common because they are the easiest to stake out and retrieve and simply depend on the fish swimming into the net and becoming entangled. Also, they can be easily used under the ice. The disadvantage is that the unwanted fish can seldom be released without gill damage and the nets must be tended regularly or the fish will die or deteriorate in quality.

Pound nets are the second most often used; they are hung on stakes and depend on fish following a lead net into a funnel-shaped heart and then into a pot or crib from which they cannot escape.

Trap nets are very much like pound nets but are designed for special locations such as channels.

Fyke nets are hoop or barrel nets; they are awkward to handle but may also be used for winter fishing under the ice. These last three types of nets are all more difficult to handle than gill nets and require at least two men to stake them out and tend them. Their advantage is that fish keep better and the unwanted fish can be returned unharmed.

Commercial trawlers were used on Big Traverse Bay of Lake of the Woods in 1961 and 1962 and from 1968 to 1970 on an experimental basis. They are not legal at this writing.

The commercial fisherman was (and is) a colorful member of the boundry waters scene. His life was not easy, and his work sometimes dangerous. He made a living but never got rich. Corporate enterprises, most of them based out east, did make money. One of the last to leave the lake region was Booth Fisheries. Most fish from the Lake of the Woods are now purchased by the Morey Fish Company of Motley, Minnesota, which operates on both the Canadian and United States sides of the lake. Alghough most commercial fishing centered around the family or functioned as partnerships, there were many "loners" on our border lakes in the early days. They were mostly bachelors and were given the name "shackers." They "squatted" where they pleased in make-shift cabins and eked out a living as fishermen and trappers.

The fishermen were as unique as the voyageurs or lumberjacks - rugged individualists, weather beaten, tough handed, and tough minded. They carved a living out of the wilderness. The remnant on Lake Superior and Lake of the Woods carry on in the best traditions of their trade.

CHAPTER TEN
The Farmer

When we think of the rugged terrain and rocky outcroppings of the Canadian Shield so characteristic of the Boundry Waters Canoe Area; it seems incongruous to talk about agriculture. Yet the Rainy River valley - particularly the Canadian side - offered some of the best farm land on the new frontier. Hundreads of settlers came to the area via railroad to Rat Portage and then steamer across Lake of the Woods and up the Rainy River between 1880 and 1900 (before the coming of the railroad to Fort Frances).

Frank Yeigh, in his "Rainy River District," included the following information for new settlers in the valley under the caption "When to go and Outfit Required":

> *The settler should if possible reach Rainy River in April or May. If he has not secured a location beforehand through one of the Government free grant agents, he should, on arrival, call upon the nearest agent, get a list of the vacant lots in the township where he desires to locate and then visit the locality and make a choice as soon as possible.*
>
> *It is somewhat difficult to state definitely the amount of capital required by the settler or immigrant who intends to make the Rainy River District his home. Having secured the Government free grant under the conditions set forth on pages 00 and 00, and having arrived at Rainy River, the prospective settler should have enough capital to erect a small and temporary log house, or a frame one if possible, building material being for sale at different points along the river where mills are situated. The approximate price of a necessary outfit might be stated as follows: For a single man, one yoke oxen, $115; plough, harrow, etc., $40; lumber, doors, windows, etc., for log house $50; provisions, $100; seed, $30; bedding, etc., $20, or say $350 in all. This sum would of course be necessarily increased in the case of a farmer with a family. For a family of five, $200 or $250 should be added to the former sum. Excellent general stores will be found at Fort Frances, Rainy River and other points where all the necessaries in the way of groceries, clothing, household utensils, etc., may be procured at reasonable prices. A general store will also be found on river lots 43 and 44 in the Township of Lash where settlers can land and get general information.[1]*

Yeigh also gives us this intriguing description of the Rainy River District in 1891 as presented by the Honorable Arthur S. Hardy, Commissioner of Crown Lands in that day, in an interview with the Toronto "Globe":

> *The crops are uniformly of the best quality, wheat running from 30 to 35 and 40 bushels per acre, and other grains in proportion. Indian corn and tomatoes ripen,*

[1]Yeigh, Frank, 1860, "The Rainy River District," Warnick and Sons, Toronto.

and the whole section, it is said, is free from the summer frosts that afflict Manitoba and the Northwest. I have never seen early settlers more comfortable. There is a chance too for the farmer at certain periods of the year, if he chooses, to engage with the lumbermen operating on Rainy Lake and Rainy River at from $1.50 to $1.75 per day, and many settlers earn money in this way. A number of excellent settlers from Muskoka have gone in this year and their work of clearing has already begun. Some of them have erected houses and others are preparing to do so. They are an excellent class of men for this district, as they have been used to clearing woodland and breaking it up. I predict a rush of settlers to this section of the country as soon as its merits are even half understood. The land is free grant land, and any settler can obtain 160 acres by settling and making the necessary improvements."

"Is Rainy River itself attractive or navigable throughout?" asked the reporter.

"It is one of the great rivers of the country. I had but a very imperfect conception of it. It appears from casual observation to be from a quarter to in some places a third of a mile wide, is almost uniform in width from source to mouth, and tugs and steamers ply over its whole course. There are but two places where navigation is difficult, viz., two comparatively small rapids about halfway up. The expenditure of a few thousand dollars would overcome all difficulty in so far as these are concerned, and make as fine a navigable river as is to be found on the continent. The volume of water is great, the current is moderate and the banks of the river beautiful throughout. One drawback is that the American border is as yet an unbroken wilderness. The accounts vary as to the farming land on the American side, but it appeared from the steamer very similar to that on the Canadian side, except that the soil is not so rich, indeed is much lighter in some places. What the Canadian section wants is roads, more ready access to the front and to existing railways, and for some of their products a more ready market, but above all what is wanted is more settlers. For all their coarse products—hay, fodder, potatoes, etc.—a ready market is found among the lumbermen at excellent prices. The settlers are looking for the rapid prosecution of the Port Arthur Railway, which it is thought must ultimately reach them and traverse the Rainy River valley."

"What about Fort Frances? Is it a settlement of any importance?"

"I was surprised to find quite a village at this point—stores, churches, schools, hotels, etc.—and I was told that at certain portions of the year business is very brisk. The village is built on the strip of land lying between Rainy Lake and the head of navigation on Rainy River, and as a site is most commanding and beautiful. The landmarks connected with the old survey of the town plot at Fort Frances have been largely obliterated, and at the request of the Council and citizens I have directed a new survey."

"Did you extend your visit to Rainy Lake?"

"Yes, we went out some miles upon the lake. It is a very fine body of water, comparing favorably with one of the most beautiful lakes on the continent—the Lake of the Woods. It is in many respects very similar, dotted with beautiful islands, but navigable in every direction. Some of the finest tracts of timber owned by the Government in the west are to be found upon the shores of and tributary to the Lake of the Woods."

"What about the lock partially built by Mr. Mackenzie at Fort Frances?"

"A comparatively small expenditure upon this lock would make navigation continuous from Rat Portage, across the Lake of the Woods, up Rainy River and through into Rainy Lake—a distance of nearly 300 miles. The lock is nearly built and the water rushes through it, but the appliances for making it useful have not been supplied. Precisely how much it would cost I am not prepared to say, but its completion would be of great assistance to lumbermen and the lumber interests, but ultimately it is thought by the people of Fort Frances it must be completed."

> *"What of the rest of the county in the Rainy River district? Is there any farming land to be found?"*
>
> *"It is not a farming country. Different accounts, however, are given upon this point. Generally it may be said the district is a mining and timber district, with parcels of land here and there capable of being converted to agricultural uses."*
>
> *"What kind of country does the Port Arthur & Western Railway pass through?"*
>
> *"I was delighted to find that the railway, quite contrary to my expectations, passes through some very rich farming land. The valley of the Kaministiquia, and further west and south of the Whitefish Valley, show some as fine soil as is to be found in many of the finest counties of the Province. We saw here and there crops growing indicating great fertility and productive capacity. The great want is agricultural settlers. The railway has revealed and practically opened to the public this large district. The road seems to have been built with skill and judgment, and ran as smoothly as many roads long completed. Messrs. Conmee and Middleton have been exceedingly energetic and are looked upon as benefactors of the district by the people at large. As the road proceeds, it reaches and runs through some of the richest iron producing districts in the Dominion and it is thought it will ultimately prove a great mineral road. Our visit to the silver mines was full of interest, as was that to Kakabeka Falls. These latter will yet become the great resort of western tourists. They are as striking in some of their features as Niagara, and it is a wonder that more has not been said and written respecting them."*

Agriculture remains an important part of the Rainy River economy to this day. Small grains are the dominant crops and beef cattle the most important livestock.

When we think of the heroes of the frontier, we seldom think of the farmer. But it was the farmer who opened the land, grubbed out the stumps, and supplied the food and fiber to nourish and clothe a growing nation. He was a pioneer in every sense of the word. Movies, television, and novels have made legends of the rancher and his cowboys, but the early Minnesota or Ontario farmer worked just as hard and faced at least as many risks (even of life and limb) as he settled the new land. Tilling the virgin soil, finding markets for his produce, fighting insects in the summer and bitter cold in the winter, protecting livestock in a wolf-infested wilderness - meant that he had to be some kind of man, and his wife, some kind of woman!

Flailing Grain - no threshing machines in the border country at the turn of the century   Courtesy Minnesota Historical Society

CHAPTER ELEVEN
Communities of the
Border Country

BAUDETTE

Because the community is located at the confluence of the Baudette and Rainy Rivers and is so close to the Lake of the Woods, it was probably an Indian village site from time to time over the centuries. The first white man to see the river banks on which Baudette grew, was no doubt Jacques De Noyon, the discoverer of Lake of the Woods. We know that he came to the Lake via the Rainy River route. The LaVèren-dryes, De la Nove, the voyageurs, and many others also passed this way before the white man's village was built here.

When the railroad came to the south end of the Lake in 1890, sawmills sprang up all the way from Rainy Lake to Warroad and Baudette was born as another "lumber town." It was not incorporated as a village until 1906. Today it is a thriving community of more than 1600 population and serves as the county seat of Lake of the Woods County (Minnesota's youngest and most sparsely settled county).

Baudette is still served by the Canadian National Railway, which enters the United States at this point and re-enters Canada at Warroad. The railroad has been servicing the area since 1890 - before Baudette was incorporated as a village.

The village was almost entirely destroyed by fire in 1910 and there were so many casualties that there was a mass burial in a trench. It is difficult today to realize what a threat forest fires were to the early villages located in the heavily timbered areas of North America. Actually, dozens of these towns and hundreds of farm buildings were "wiped out" by raging fires early in this century. the death toll was often heavy. Devastating fires swept through thousands of acres of Lake of the Woods timber in 1734, 1803-04, 1894, and 1910.

As a gateway to the south end of the Lake of the Woods, Baudette has become a tourist center. However, the economy of the village is also dependent on Rowell Laboratories, the U.S. Air Force Radar Station, agriculture, and logging.

The Rowell Laboratories were founded in 1929 by the late T.H. Rowell, a pharmacist. Rowell's father was a commercial fisherman and Ted was familiar with the Lake's large population of burbot.[1] He was aware that it was a fresh water cousin of the ocean codfish. Rowell learned to extract the vitamin rich oil from the large fish livers

[1] A rough fish sometimes called eel-pout lawyer or ling cod and the sole surviving fresh water species of the codfish family.

and found a national market for his product. In those days the children of the northern climates of the world were fortified against colds by generous doses of cod liver oil (a horrible tasting liquid which usually required a "chaser" of jelly or some other sweet, but actually a good source of Vitamins A & D). With the coming of World War II the national supply dried up and the burbot of the Lake of the Woods became the source of the "missing" vitamins. Today, the liver extract is relatively a small part of the business, as Rowell laboratories manufactures a great variety of pharmaceutical products for world wide distribution. The company specializes in preparations for clinics and University hospitals. It is not a little suprising to find such an industry on the very edge of the wilderness. It's success is a real tribute to the Rowell family and the nearly 100 employees who have contributed to its growth.

First aerial view of Baudette, about 1916.   Courtesy James Tabour

Ted Rowell, Sr., the founder of the company, was also chairman of the committee that worked long and tirelessly for the construction of the International Bridge across the Rainy River - joining the twin cities of Baudette, Minnesota, and Rainy River, Ontario. The bridge was constructed in 1960 and was made possible by federal support resulting from legislation introduced by U.S. Senator Edward J. Thye (R. - Minn.) in 1958.

Prior to 1960 a ferry service was operated during the open water seasons and cars crossed on the ice in winter.

Agriculture, another bulwark of the Baudette economy, contributes about one and a half million dollars annually to that economy through the sale of farm products. The soil is quited fertile and crops such as wheat, oats, barley, rye, flax, red and sweet clover seed, timothy seed, and potatoes for seed have been found suitable to the cool climate and relatively short growing season.

Timber products contribute another million dollars annually to the Baudette economy. Two lumber and wood products plants are located in nearby Williams. Although the village of Williams is not on the Lake, it is the gateway to Zippel Bay State Park[1] which is on the south shore of the Lake of the Woods.

A United States Air Force Radar Station, once located just south of the city, contributed much to the business community. It was established in 1959. An expansion of the facility in 1969 when it became a BUIC III site, increased employment to about 250 military personnel. It is now in the process of being abandoned.

A tool and die shop which also specializes in metal stampings (the Wabanica Products Company) is also located in Baudette.

Originally, a separate village known as "Spooner," was located across the Baudette River. It was incorporated as part of the village of Baudette in 1954. It was in Spooner that the great Shevin - Mathieu Mill was established in 1905. Here 60 million board feet of lumber was processed annually and 350 men were employed on a double shift. The mill was destroyed by fire in 1921.

ELY

Named for Samuel P. Ely, who was prominent in the development of mining in the area, the community owes its origin to the high grade iron deposits of the Vermilion Range. The discovery of ore in 1886 set off a flury of activity. A townsite was platted the following spring and the very next year (1888) marked the arrival of the Duluth and Iron Range Railroad (now a part of the Duluth Messabe, and Iron Range Railroad). The first shipment of ore was made in 1889. Ely received its charter as a city in 1891 and the 1910 census - only 24 years after the discovery of ore - revealed a population of 3572!

Ely mines were of the underground variety (in contrast to "open pit") and plunged as far as 1600 feet below ground level.

The opening of the mines was followed almost imediately by the arrival of the lumberjacks, and logging remains an important part of the economy to this day. Ely is a headquarters for the U.S. Forest Service and is surrounded by the Superior National Forest - a creation of the Theodore Roosevelt administration.

Recreation is Ely's newest industry. Located on the very doorstep of our **Canoe Country**, the community is the most important gateway to the Boundary Waters Canoe Area Wilderness. It serves as a supply base for canoeists, outfitters and resorts of the region.

Few communities in this land are so blessed with natural resources, including mineral deposits (iron, zinc, copper, nickel and others), forests, and an abundance of lakes, streams and recreation potential. But the blessings have also brought frustration. Federal legislation has given wilderness preservation a higher priority than mining or logging, thus curtailing their considerable economic potential. Meanwhile, the relatively short tourist season is not sufficient to sustain a healthy economy year around. Conflict - often bitter - has been the inevitable result.

[1]The Zippel family were pioneers in commercial fishing on the Lake of the Woods.

Corduroy logging road between Erie Lake and Ely   Courtesy Minnesota Historical Society

FORT FRANCES

Strategically located on the canoe route from the East, at the west end of Rainy Lake, the site became a natural stopping place for explorers, voyageurs, fur traders, missionaries and early settlers. The coming of roads and the construction of the international bridge (1912) made the community the major port of entry between Minnesota and Ontario.

Jacques de Noyon, the first white man to discover the Lake of the Woods, headquartered in this area. LaVèrendye's first fort (St. Pierre) was erected by his nephew (La Jemeraye) in the vicinity of what is now Pither's Point in 1731.

A missionary once described Rainy Lake as a gathering place of -

> *Generally from two to five thousand Indians in the immediate vicinity of the company's fort; and during a part of the year, their numbers may be estimated at not less than 2000. Rainy Lake is one of the principal places in the country for holding the Great Medicine Feasts.*

In 1793 the Northwest Trading Company built a compound at Fort Frances below the falls and named it Fort Lac La Pluie. The very next year Duncan McGillvray visited the fort and described what was perhaps the first labor dispute in the West. It had to do with a strike by some men of the "fur brigades" against the trading company.

> *A few dicontented persons in their band, wishing to do as much mischief as possible, assembled their companions together several times on the voyage outward and presented to them how much their interest suffered by the passing obedience to the will of their masters, when their ability to the company might ensure them not only of better treatment, but of many other conditions which they would prescribe with Spirit and Resolution.*
>
> *. . . They all declared with one voice that unless their wages would be augmented, and several other conditions equally unreasonable, granted them, they would immediately set off to Montreal. . .yet, a timidity was observed in their behavior which proved very fortunate for their masters, who took good advantage of them and before night prevailed on a few of the most timid to return to their duty, and the rest being ashamed to abandon their companions, soon followed the example. . .a few of the most resolute were obstinate enough to hold out. . .and were therefore sent to Montreal in disgrace.*

In 1825, following the merger of the Northwest Company with the Hudson's Bay Company, the governor of the new conglamorate, George Simpson, visited the fort with his bride, Frances Ramsey Simpson. The result was the renaming of the fort in honor of the young Mrs. Simpson, hence: Fort Frances.

The "fort" burned in 1874 but was restored and served as a trading post until 1897 or 1898. About that time it ceased to be a fur trading center and was used only as a retail outlet unitl it was destroyed again by fire in 1903, and never replaced.

Following the fur trading era, lumbering became the chief industry. Wood and wood products remain the chief factor in the community's economy. Initially, the logs were floated to Rat Portage at the north end of the Lake of the Woods. The coming of the Canadian Northern Railroad in 1902 resulted in sawmills from Rainy Lake all the way down the river and along the south shore of the Lake of the Woods as far as Warroad. Actually, a few mills were opened on Rainy River as early as 1890.

The dam at Koochiching Falls was built over a five year period from 1905-1910. Its completion provided the opportunity for power and the coming of the paper industry. The Fort Frances Paper Mill was in operation by 1914. The original ownership was forced into receivership in 1931 and was subsequently taken over by the Minnesota Ontario Paper Company which in turn was purchased by Boise Cascade in 1965. A new kraft mill was constructed in 1970-71.

The international bridge, which joined Fort Frances with International Falls in 1912, was originally constructed so that the first portion could be raised to allow the passage of steamboats. When the dream of a canal system joining Lake Superior with Lake of the Woods vanished, the bridge was rebuilt.

Farming has been a major part of the economy since the early 1890's, long before the land on the Minnesota side of the Rainy River was cultivated. In 1876, 20 townships in the area were surveyed and parceled out in 160 acre lots to settlers free of charge. They were allowed to purchase an additional 80 acres of adjoining land at $1 per acre.

The town of Fort Frances was incorporated on April 11, 1903. Previously it had been a part of the Municipality of Alberton (1891-1903). This area was a part of the disputed territory claimed by both Ontario and Manitoba between 1859 and 1871. Fort Frances has been a part of the territorial district of Rainy River since 1909, and has been the center of the Provincial Judicial District serving that area since that time.

In addition to industry and agriculture, Fort Frances is well established as a gateway to one of the finest wilderness and recreation areas of Canada.

Hudson's Bay Trading Post at Fort Frances (1902)   Courtesy Minnesota Historical Society

GRAND MARAIS ("GREAT MARSH")

The first white men to settle at Grand Marais were traders, and it is believed they used the harbor as a base for their operations as early as 1775. However, it was not established as a village until nearly 100 years later in 1871. In 1854 the trading post was operated by a man named Godfrey; he also became the first postmaster when an office was established in 1856.

Henry Mayhew and Sam Howenstine and their families were the pioneers who developed the village site and opened a general store; they also became the managers of the post office.

The community has been involved in commercial fishing from the beginning; but sports fishing now makes a much larger contribution to the economy.

Mining also had its impact and it is believed the famous Gunflint Trail began as a wagon road to the Paulson mine. Legend also tells us that the mining road was preceded by an Indian trail.

Logging and lumbering have been a major part of the economy since the founding of the village and they continue to make a significant contribution.

Today, Grand Marias is one of the major focal points for tourism on the north shore of Lake Superior and is a "jumping off place" to *Canoe Country.*

Grand Marais in 1894   Courtesy Minnesota Historical Society

GRAND PORTAGE ("THE GREAT CARRYING PLACE")

Grand Portage may have been the earliest White settlement in Minnesota. We believe that Duluth stopped here in 1679 others may have used the location as a base of operations from that time on. It is likely that there was a post on this site in LaVèrendye's day (the 1730's); he was the first to make a written record of using the Grand Portage trail. The location on the largest indentation on the Minnesota shore of Lake Superior, adjacent to the trail leading to the **Boundary Waters** route, made Grand Portage an ideal site for a settlement.

The first British traders arrived in 1762 following the takeover of the region by the British from the French. In 1766 or shortly thereafter, John Askin is thought to have cleared the site for the construction of the great North West Company fort. Jonathan Carver visited here in 1767 in the hope of replenishing his supplies from white traders he expected would be there. He found no whites but, instead, about 300 "friendly" Indians. Later, voyageurs and traders did come that way on their return from the west but had no surplus of supplies to share. Carver was forced to return east along with them via Lake Superior.

By the time of the American Revolution, Grand Portage had surpassed Fort William as a center of trading activity on Lake Superior and the huge North West fort was constructed in 1788 (and abandoned in 1803). A replica of the fort may be seen today at Grand Portage. Several descriptions have survived of the fort at its prime. The stockade enclosed 16 buildings, the most important of which were painted or trimmed in "Spanish brown." Their roofs were of cedar or pine shingles, in contrast to the thatched bows used on more temporary buildings on the frontier. The Great Hall was the most important building and it was here where meals were served and the historic trading and negotiating took place. The gates of the fort were closed at night and sentries posted - more to watch for fire than some human enemy.

Other forts and posts were erected at Grand Portage, particularly during its "hey day." We know that in 1802 there was a smaller stockade known as "Boucher's Fort" and the tents of the X Y Company were set up between that post and the North West Company stockade. The X Y Company also had a post near Fort Charlotte on the Pigeon River at the other end of the portage.

In 1800, the United States tax collector arrived and served notice that duty would be charged on goods brought in from Canada starting the next year. The British responded by moving their operations north to Fort William (Thunder Bay) and thereafter used the Kaministiquia River route to Rainy Lake. However, the British did continue some operations at Grand Portage until after the War of 1812 - on which occasion Lt. Thomas Bennett occupied the site with a garrison to protect it against a possible American invasion.

Canoe Building   Courtesy Minnesota Historical Society

The voyageurs preferred the Grand Portage route. The more northern route had more swampy portages and a seemingly greater infestation of insects.

From 1802 to 1830, there were several small, independent operations under license from the United States government. In the 1830's and 40's, John Jacob Astor's American Fur Company was on the scene but was more involved in commercial fishing (on Lake Superior) than fur trading.

In 1838, that spiritual giant, Father Pierz, started a Catholic school and mission here. In 1856, Grand Portage was recognized with its own post office. A wharf was constucted in the 1780's. Sailing vessels out of Sault Ste. Marie had made Grand Portage a port of call starting with the American revolution.

The Ojibway Village at Grand Portage kept itself quite separate from other Chippewa bands and over the early years developed close ties with the British, even after their trading operations were moved north to Fort William in the early 1800's. The village was ignored as the U.S. Government signed treaties with all other American

Ojibway and it wasn't until 1854 that the Grand Portage Indians had their own Treaty. After that date they were more closely affiliated with the other Minnesota and Wisconsin bands and identified with the United States. The population of the village varied over the years. Schoolcraft reported 60 "some" in 1828 and 50 in 1832. By 1940, however, the community had increased to 135.

Although Grand Portage has been in use by the white man since 1669, and by the Indian for unknown generations, the peak of activity was over a twenty-five year period during the last part of the 18th Century, when a thousand or more voyageurs and perhaps twice that many Indians gathered in rendezvous each July (pages 4 and 5 of Chapter III). The arrival of the voyageurs must have been dramatic. It was the custom of the "pork eaters" to stop short of the bay and dress in their finest and most gaudy clothing. Then with paddles swinging in time to a favorite chanty, they rounded the last point and approached the beach.

The setting was then much as it is now, the bay framed by two points, "Hat" and "Raspberry," with Mutton Island lying at the entrance. As the voyageurs entered the bay they were greeted by a panarama of bustling trading posts, tents and Indian lodges with Sugar Loaf Mountain as the back-drop for the great North West Fort. Since about 70 canoes were manufactured by the Indians here each year, there were probably several under construction at any one time to replace those battered by the rugged journey. It is difficult to imagine a more exciting or colorful frontier settlement. Grand Portage is a National Historic site and was established as a National Monument in 1960.

Great Hall at Grand Portage restored (1975 Photo)

INTERNATIONAL FALLS

The first white settler to build on the location of present day International Falls was a Scottish prospector named Alexander Baker. He arrived on the scene in 1870 after paddling all the way from Lake Superior and chose a site overlooking Koochiching Falls for the construction of his log cabin. Here he lived until his death September 14, 1899, at the age of 72. The tract of land to which he laid claim included much of the present day Mando Paper Mill site and some of the business district and residential area. Because this part of Minnesota had not been surveyed, it took ten years to clear the title to the homestead.

C.J. Rockwood, of Minneapolis, bought all of the Baker claim with the exception of the one acre on which the cabin was located (Baker's Acre) for $6000 in 1892. He had recognized the water power potential of the falls. Rockwood, in turn, sold out in 1900 to E.W. Backus and W.F. Brooks, who were already well established in the lumber business in Minnesota.

Joseph Baker, a nephew of the founder of the village, arrived from Scotland in 1881. He was destined to become the first postmaster, the first bandmaster, and the first Justice of the Peace of Koochiching (the original name for International Falls).

Milestones in the history of the village include:

> *1894 - The construction of the first school with L.A. Ogaard as the teacher.*
>
> *1901 - Construction of the Canadian Railroad to Fort Frances.*
>
> *1902 - A fire very nearly destroyed the entire village.*
>
> *1903 - Dr. M.E. Withrow established his medical practice.*
>
> *1904 - R.S. McDonald arrived from Grand Rapids and cleared 240 acres of land which was soon to become part of the townsite.*
>
> *1905 - A contract was let for the construction of the dam. A wagon and footbridge was completed. A telephone exchange became operational with sixty instruments.*
>
> *1907 - The Minnesota and International Railroad and the Duluth Winnipeg and Pacific reached the border town.*
>
> *1910, 1911 - Insulate was first produced.*
>
> *1914 - The manufacture of paper was begun.*
>
> *1939-40 - Plant Mix Bituminous surface applied to gravel highways leading into town 1½ inches. [Some oil treatment in previous years]*

A 1906 edition of the International Falls Echo boasted of a business community which included -

four general stores	*1 feed store*
four lawyers	*1 blacksmith shop*
two barbar shops	*2 tailor shops*

Athough International Falls had a reputation as a "rough and lively border town," the first murder was not recorded until 1907. The killing was the result of a quarrel between two black men.

Before the coming of the railroad, travel was extremely difficult in this part of the world. We are told of one family which moved with all their worldly possessions (about a railroad car full) from New Prague, Minnesota, to Koochiching in 1894. They first

Main Street, International Falls, 1929   Courtesy Minnesota Historical Society

traveled by railroad to Duluth. There they transferred with their goods to a freight boat and headed for Port Arthur (Thunder Bay). At Port Arthur they again unloaded and boarded the Canadian Pacific Railroad for Rat Portage (Kenora). Here, all their goods were transferred to boats in which they crossed the Lake of the Woods. They then journeyed up the Rainy River to Fort Frances. A few weeks later they crossed the river to Koochiching. The journey from New Prague to Fort Frances took fifteen days and included loading and unloading all their possessions four times!

Koochiching Rapids from the Canadian side, 1901   Courtesy Minnesota Historical Society

Before the coming of the railroad in 1907, travel, whenever possible was by boat in summer and dog team in winter, however, it was often necessary or more practical to simply cut across country from such cities as Bemidji, Grand Rapids, or Big Falls (then called Ripple) - the latter served as terminal point for the M and I railroad from 1905 to 1907. The trails were often poorly marked and led across huge bogs and a dozen or more streams. Hoards of flies and mosquitoes were an added threat in summer and cold and snow were the enemies during the winter months. Althought there is no authenticated record of wolves attacking or killing these early travelers, they often followed them and were at least a psychological threat!

Travelers from Duluth and the Iron Range towns of Minnesota could go by rail as far as Tower and then portage to Harding on Crane Lake, from where they could travel the remainder of the journey by water.

As we journey by air or by auto through this area today, we can scarcely imagine the hardships endured by these early travelers. Next time you drive from Blackduck to Baudette or International Falls, try to visualize *walking* across those huge bogs or through the dark cedar swamps!

VILLAGE OF RAINY RIVER

Located across the river from Baudette, the village of Rainy River is the gateway to Canada for those visiting southern and western Sabaskong Bay of Lake of the Woods or the eastern approach to Big Traverse. It is joined to Baudette by a toll bridge which was constructed in 1960; prior to that date a ferry service was operated on the river by Frank Watson.

The Hudson's Bay Company operated a post not far from the village site near the mouth of the Rainy River most of the time from 1794 to 1893. It was originally constructed by H.B.C. employee Thomas Norn, and occupied the next year by John McKay, who described the post as being located on "one of the beautifulest river I ever saw in this country." Just two years later, McKay and his men were transferred to the Red River area. In 1798, the Hudson's Bay Company sent John Cobb to "the McKay Hall," but when he arrived he found that employees of the Northwest Trading Company had plundered the post and burned down "the men's house." Because of the severe competition from the French, the post was not again occupied until 1826. In later years (after 1832) it was referred to as "Hungry Hall." (see pages 12 and 13, Chapter II.)

The village of Rainy River had its beginnings as a saw mill town and was first called "Beaver Mill." The Rainy River Lumber Company had a large operation here from the turn-of-the-century to 1911, when it was dismantled. In 1913, Shevlin-Clarke, Ltd. erected a mill. Both operations were located here because of the coming of the railroad (at the start of the century) and the Canadian National is still a major employer. Logging and lumbering also remain important to the community while agriculture, tourism, and the Arctic Cat Industry help diversify the economy. Although most tourists who enter Canada through the village of Rainy River are headed for the Lake of the Woods area, the river itself - from which the community takes its name - is a magnificent stream and a real asset. John McDonald, a clerk and trader with the Hudson's Bay Company, said of Rainy River, "This is deemed the most beautiful river in the Northwest."

What a privilege to use the very same portages as the explorers, traders, and voyageurs

The Boundary Waters still abound with wildlife   Both pictures courtesy Minneapolis YMCA

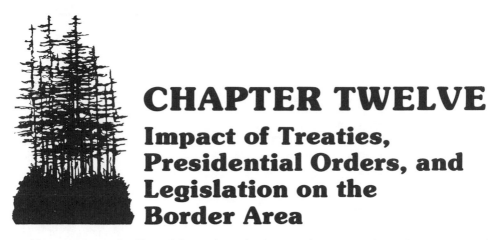

CHAPTER TWELVE
Impact of Treaties, Presidential Orders, and Legislation on the Border Area

Few regions in the United States have had so much attention from Congress and the Executive Branch as our *Canoe Country*. This is also true, but to a lesser extent, of the Canadian Quetico. Because the area is so rich in timber and mineral resources and also has so much to offer in the way of recreation and natural beauty and since it is so difficult to have the best of both of these worlds, it is not surprising that Congress and Parliament have been drawn into the resulting controversies again and again. Legislation and the resulting regulations have filled volumes. This chapter will highlight the landmark actions, but there are many more pieces of legislation or executive orders which indirectly have had an effect on the region. The legislation and resulting regulations have become more and more protective and restrictive down through the years.

WEBSTER ASHBURTON TREATY - 1842.

As indicated in Chapter IV, the Minnesota-Ontario border was established by the Treaty of Paris in 1783, following the Revolutionary War. The language specified that the line from Lake Superior west should follow "the usual water communication to Lake of the Woods, thence through said lake to the most northwest part thereof, and from thence on a due west course to the river Mississippi." As we stated in that chapter, this became an impossibility because the "Father of Waters" does not start that far north. In 1823, commissioners representing both the United States and British governments were active in the region, trying to mark out the border. They were limited in their work by the fact that there had been no agreement on which was the "usual water communication" between Lake Superior and the Lake of the Woods. The Treaty of Ghent, following the War of 1812, had addressed the problem of relating the Lake of the Woods to the Mississippi River, by simply stating that the 49th parallel would be the boundary west of the Lake. Thus it was left to Daniel Webster, representing the United States, and Lord Ashburton, representing Her Majesties Government, to work out a treaty specifying the border form Lake Superior to Lake of the Woods. Webster argued that the Kaministiquia River route from Thunder Bay west was the usual route of travel to Lake of the Woods; Ashburton insisted it was the Pigeon River route out of Grand Portage. The British position prevailed, perhaps because that government had yielded on their earlier proposal that the border should be drawn from Lake Superior to the source of the Mississippi, and then west. The Webster-Ashburton Treaty also specified: "It being understood that all water communications and all the usual portages along the line from Lake Superior to the Lake of the Woods and also Grand Portage, from the shore of Lake Superior to the Pigeon River, as now actually used, shall be free and open to the use of citizens and subjects of both countries."

THE ORGANIC ACT of 1849.

This legislation created the Territory of Minnesota and reserved sections 16 and 36 in each township for school purposes. This has raised the issue of what shall be done about those sections in the BWCA now that they are not available for sale or commercial use or development.

THE ENABLING ACT of 1857.

Minnesota statehood was authorized by this act and it reaffirmed that sections 16 and 36 in each township were to be retained for school purposes.

AMERICAN ANTIQUITIES ACT of 1906.

A permit from the Secretary of Agriculture is necessary, as a result of this legislation, to "appropriate, excavate, injure, or destroy any historic or prehistoric ruin or monument." The Boundary Waters is so steeped in history, this act is indeed important to the area.

ROOT-BRYCE TREATY of 1909.

Article II of this treaty provided for the establishment of an International Joint Commission of the United States and Canada for the purpose of having jurisdiction over all matters involving the "use, diversion, or obstruction of the boundary water." It is composed of six commissioners, three from each country. The commission is active and issues regular reports. Appointments are paid, part-time positions

WEEKS ACT of 1911.

This legislation established a National Forest Reservation Commission to consider and approve the purchase of lands for National forest purposes. The Secretary of Agriculture was authorized to actually purchase those tracts recommended by the commission. He was also authorized to exchange federal lands for additions to the designated forests or the private owner could be given a permit by the Secretary to harvest timber on federal lands in exchange for the property. This act was amplified by the LAND EXCHANGE ACT of 1922 which authorized the Secretary to trade properties or timber rights with private landowners within the designated boundaries of a National Forest. Additional legislation, passed in 1911, gave the Secretary of Agriculture the right to grant permits to private parties to use up to 80 acre tracts of federal land for "providing facilities for public recreation, convenience, or safety" - for up to thirty years at a time.

The FEDERAL POWER COMMISSION ACT of 1920.

Not only was the Federal Power Commission created by this act, but the commission was authorized to issue leases across navigable waters and public lands for the "development, transmission, and utilization of power."

The KNUTSON-VANDENBURG ACT of 1930.

Authored by Congressman Harold Knutson of Minnesota and Arthur Vandenburg of Michigan, this act authorized a surcharge on timber sales from Federal lands for the purpose of reforestation.

The SHIPSTEAD-NEWTON-NOLAN ACT of 1930.

Minnesota's Senator Shipstead promoted this most significant legislation which effected Lake, Cook, and St. Louis counties. It provided that within those counties, natural water levels should be preserved, no logging should take place within 400 feet of shorelines, the wilderness nature of shorelines would be preserved, and federal lands would no longer be available for sale.

The CIVIL AERONAUTICS ACT of 1938.

This legislation was important to the Boundary Waters area because it established federal control of all air space above the United States, including the space over lakes and streams. This gave the President of the United States the authority to limit air travel over the BWCA, such as in President Truman's executive order issued in 1949 which prohibited air traffic under 4000 feet over certain portions of this region.

The THYE-BLATNIK ACT of 1948.

This landmark legislation authorized the Secretary of Agriculture to acquire by purchase and/or condemnation those lands and improvements thereon which might "impair or threaten to impair" specific portions of the Boundary Waters wilderness area. Thye and Blatnik developed personal interests in this region when they were Governor and State Senator, respectively, and they carried these interests to fruition when they became members of Congress.

The THYE-HUMPHREY-BLATNIK-ANDERSEN ACT of 1956.

Senators Thye and Humphrey and Congressmen Blatnik and Andersen (all of Minnesota) authored legislation expanding the area wherein property and improvements could be purchased and/or condemned by the Department of Agriculture and increased the appropriations for the purpose to $2,500,000 - as compared to $500,000 in the 1948 bill. In 1961, an additional $2,000,000 was appropriated.

The WILDERNESS ACT of 1964.

A National wilderness preservation system was established. It was so worded as to include the BWCA, but it was also made clear that nothing in that act would diminish the effect of previous legislation concerning this region.

The NATIONAL ENVIRONMENTAL POLICY ACT of 1969.

This legislation had an effect on all parts of the United States in that it provided for an environmental impact study and statement wherever federal legislation or actions were involved. Naturally, this also applied to the BWCA.

VOYAGEURS NATIONAL PARK, created by Congress in 1969.

Although authored by all of Minnesota's congressional delegation (McCarthy, Mondale, Blatnik, Quie, Nelsen, Zwach, Langen, Frazer, and Karth), the concept was developed and promoted by former Governor Elmer L. Andersen and endorsed by resolution of both houses of the Minnesota Legislature. This is not to say it was without controversy - far from it. The park includes most of Rainy Lake, part of Namekan, all of Kabetogama and other lakes east to the BWCA. It includes many points of historical interest as well as a vast recreational region. In topography and beauty it is very similar to the rest of the Boundary Waters. The area is 219,000 acres as compared to the 1,075,500 acres in the BWCA Wilderness.

BOUNDARY WATERS CANOE AREA WILDERNESS ACT - 1978.

Perhaps the most controversial of all legislation effecting the Boundary Waters, the Wilderness Act designated approximately 1,075,500 acres as BWCA "Wilderness," provided for the further purchase of private properties within that area, gave the Department of Agriculture the right of "first refusal" on the sale of private properites on certain lakes in the area once one piece of property has been sold to the Federal Government, substantially expanded the restrictions on the use of motor boats and snowmobiles, added further restrictions on logging, and further restricted the exploration for or mining of minerals. The Act also established a Boundary Waters Canoe Area Mining Protection Area of approximately 222,000 acres. The Secretary of Agriculture is authorized to acquire the mineral rights of private parties (other than the State of Minnesota) within the Wilderness and Mining Protection areas. Recreation programs and resources are to be expanded - such as hiking and cross-country ski trails.

Federal regulations resulting from all this legislation has brought about even more specific controls in many areas, including mining, mineral explorations, logging, motor boats, use of pack and riding animals, wildlife management, fire prevention, use of power saws, camping, and entry to the area itself. It must be remembered that the Canadian government has also legislated similar (but not as restrictive) controls of the Quetico area.

The State of Minnesota also has had considerable legislation concerning the BWCA Wilderness; mostly in response to and in cooperation with federal laws. Most recently (1979), an Advisory Committee on the BWCA was established (appointed by the Governor).

And the end is not in sight!

BIBLIOGRAPHY

Bigsby, John, Notes on the Geography and Geology of Lake Superior, John Murray, London, 1825.

Bishop, Charles A., The Northern Ojibwa and the Fur Trade, Holt Reinhart, and Winston, Toronto, 1974.

Bolz, J. Arnold, Portage Into the Past, Lund Press, Minneapolis, 1975.

Boundary Waters Canoe Area Review Committee Report to the Secretary of Agriculture, Duluth, 1965.

Bryce, George, The Lake of the Woods, its History, Geology, Mining, and Manufacturing, Manitoba Fress Press, 1897.

Beyner, Robert, Boundary Waters Canoe Area, Wilderness Press, Berkley California, 1978.

Colum, Padsaic, The Voyageurs, Macmillan, New York, 1925.

Fritzen, John, Lake Superior, St. Louis County Historical Society, 1974.

Gillispie, C. W., The Voyageur, Folklore and Legend, Reed City, Michigan, 1968 (?).

Heinselman, Miron L., Outline History of the Boundary Waters Canoe Area, Friends of the Boundary Waters, 1976.

Johnson, Elder, Aspects of Upper Great Lakes Anthropology, Minnesota Historical Society, St. Paul, 1974.

Kaups, Nathin, North Shore Commercial Fishing, 1849-1870, "Minnesota History," Summer, 1978.

Martinson, David, A Long Time Ago is Just Like Today, Duluth Indian Education Advisory Committee, Duluth, 1976.

Nute, Grace, Caesars of the Wilderness, Appleton, Century Co., New York, 1943.
    Lake Superior, Bobbs, Merrill Co., 1944
    Rainy Lake Country, Minnesota Historical Society, St. Paul, 1943
    Rainy River Country, Minnesota Historical Society, St. Paul, 1950
    Vayageurs Highway, Minnesota Historical Society, St. Paul, 1941

Oliphant, Laurence, Minnesota and the Far West, Blackwood and Sons, Edinburgh and London, 1855.

Searle, R. Newele, A Land Set Apart.

Tanner, John, An Indian Captivity, California State Library, from original narrative dictated in 1830.

Taylor, Lolita, Ojibwa, the Wild Rice People, Wisconsin Indianhead VTAE Report, 1976.

Wheeler, R. C., Kenyon, W.A., Woolworth, A.R., and Birk, D., Voices From the Rapids, Minnesota Historical Society, St. Paul, 1973.

Yeigh, Frank, "The Rainy River District," Warnik & Sons, Toronto, 1860.

NOTES

NOTES

Other Books by Duane R. Lund

Andrew, Youngest Lumberjack
A Beginner's Guide to Hunting and Trapping
A Kid's Guidebook to Fishing Secrets
Early Native American Recipes and Remedies
Fishing and Hunting Stories from The Lake of the Woods
Lake of the Woods, Yesterday and Today, Vol. 1
Lake of the Woods, Earliest Accounts, Vol. 2
Our Historic Upper Mississippi
Tales of Four Lakes and a River
The Youngest Voyageur
White Indian Boy
Nature's Bounty for Your Table
The North Shore of Lake Superior, Yesterday and Today
Leech Lake, Yesterday and Today
Gull Lake, Yesterday and Today
150 Ways to Enjoy Potatoes
101 Favorite Freshwater Fish Recipes
101 Favorite Wild Rice Recipes
101 Favorite Mushroom Recipes
Camp Cooking, Made Easy and Fun
Sauces, Seasonings and Marinades for Fish and Wild Game
The Scandinavian Cookbook
Gourmet Freshwater Fish Recipes, Quick and Easy
The Soup Cookbook
101 Ways to Add to Your Income
The Indian Wars
Traditional Holiday Ethnic Recipes - collected all over the world
Entertainment Helpers, Quick and Easy

About the Author

- EDUCATOR (RETIRED, SUPERINTENDENT OF SCHOOLS, STAPLES, MINNESOTA);
- HISTORIAN (PAST MEMBER OF EXECUTIVE BOARD, MINNESOTA HISTORICAL SOCIETY); Past Member of BWCA and National Wilderness Trails Advisory Committees;
- SENIOR CONSULTANT to the Blandin Foundation
- WILDLIFE ARTIST, OUTDOORSMAN.